Edward Everett Hale

Ten Times One Is Ten

The Possible Reformation

Edward Everett Hale

Ten Times One Is Ten
The Possible Reformation

ISBN/EAN: 9783744709323

Printed in Europe, USA, Canada, Australia, Japan

Cover: Foto ©Lupo / pixelio.de

More available books at **www.hansebooks.com**

TEN TIMES ONE IS TEN.

TEN TIMES ONE IS TEN:

THE POSSIBLE REFORMATION.

A Story in Nine Chapters.

BY

COL. FREDERIC INGHAM.

BOSTON:
ROBERTS BROTHERS.
1871.

Entered according to Act of Congress, in the year 1870, by
ROBERTS BROTHERS,
In the Office of the Librarian of Congress at Washington.

CAMBRIDGE:
PRESS OF JOHN WILSON AND SON.

PREFACE.

THIS little book would never have been written, I suppose, but for the persuasion of my kind friend, the late Dr. WAYLAND, the President of Brown University. It is nearly fifteen years ago that I told him the plan of this story, if it may be called a story, expressing the wish that some of the masters would undertake to illustrate the lessons involved in it. Every one who knew him — and how many there are who knew him enough to love him! — will remember how practical and how personal was every notion of the religious life, of Christian labor, and of missionary triumph, in his mind. What he thought the practical and personal character of my little sketch pleased him; and he was kind enough to urge me once and again to enlarge it, and to print it. I think it is because he wished it, that I have tried to do so.

There are hundreds of people who know that the character of HARRY WADSWORTH and his unselfish influence are studied from the life.

I dedicate the book to those who knew him and loved him.

         EDWARD E. HALE.

SOUTH CONGREGATIONAL CHURCH,
  BOSTON, Sept. 17, 1870.

CONTENTS.

CHAP.		PAGE
I.	WHAT BEGAN IT	9
II.	THREE YEARS AFTER	28
III.	TEN TIMES A HUNDRED	46
IV.	TEN TIMES A THOUSAND	78
V.	EUROPE, ASIA, AFRICA, AND THE ISLES OF THE OCEAN	90
VI.	TEN TIMES A HUNDRED THOUSAND	97
VII.	THE CONFERENZ AT CHRISTMAS ISLAND	109
VIII.	TEN TIMES TEN MILLION	118
IX.	A THOUSAND MILLION	130

TEN TIMES ONE IS TEN.

CHAPTER I.

WHAT BEGAN IT.

[*A talk in Calabria, after dress parade.*]

I SUPPOSE it was the strangest Club that ever came into being.

There were these ten members I tell you of. And they have never met but this once, nor do I believe they will ever meet again.

They met in the railroad station at North Colchester, waiting for the express train. The express train, if you happen to remember that particular afternoon and evening, was five hours and twenty minutes behind time. They knew it was behind time, but they had nowhere else to go, and it was then and there that the Club was formed.

For they had all come together at Harry Wadsworth's funeral. The most manly and most womanly fellow he, whom I ever knew;

the merriest and the freshest, and the bravest and the wisest; the most sympathizing when people were sorry, and the most sympathizing when they were glad. Thunder! If I were at home, and could just show you three or four of Harry's yellow letters that lie there, then you would know something about him. Simply, he was the most spirited man who ever stumbled over me; he was possessed, and possessed with a true spirit,— that was what he was; and so he had guns enough, and more than guns enough, for any emergency.

And Harry Wadsworth had died. And from north, and east, and south, we ten there had come to the funeral. And we were waiting for the train, as I said; and that is the way the Club was born. Then and there it had its first meeting, and, as I say, its last, most likely.

Bridget Corcoran may strictly be called the founder of the Club, unless dear Harry himself was. For Bridget Corcoran was the first person that said any thing. I never can sit still very long at a time at such places. And I had sat in my chair by that overfilled stove, in that stifling room, as long as I could stand it, and a good deal longer, none of us saying any thing. Then I had gone out and walked the platform, brooding, till it seemed to me that any thing was better than walking the platform. Then I went in again to find the air just as dead and stived and insupportable as it was before. And this time I left the door open and walked across to the back window, which looked on a different wood-pile from the wood-pile the front window looked upon. I need not say that the only variety in our prospects was in our choice of wood-piles; but we could look at the ends of sticks, or at the sides of them, as we preferred.

I walked to the back window, and began looking at the back wood-pile.

"You knew Mr. Wadsworth?" said Bridget Corcoran, timidly. And it was a comfort to me.

"Knew him!" said I; "I did not know anybody else!"

"I like to tell you about him then," said she, with her pleasant Irish accent. "I like to tell every one about him. For, save for him, I do not know where I should be this day; and I do know where my boy Will would be."

"How is that?" I asked, roused up a little by her sympathy.

"Will, sir, would be in the State's Prison save for him you carried to the grave this day; and for me, I think I should have died of a broken heart. You know, your reverence, that in the charge of the freight station, when he was first appointed here, it was for him to say who should have the chips, and who should not have them. And he was so good — as he always was — as to give me the second right in the wood-yard; Mary Morris always having the first, because her husband, who is now switch-tender, lost his arm in the great smash-up come Michaelmas five years gone by. He gave me the second right, I say; and though I say it who should not, I never abused my privilege, and he knew I never did, your reverence, as how could I, when he was always so kind, and often called me into his office, and always spoke to me as kindly as if I was a born lady, as indeed he was a born gentleman."

Ah me! if I only could go on and tell Bridget's story as she told it herself, with the thousand pretty praises of dear Harry, you would better understand what manner of man he was, and how the Club was born. But there is no time for that, and this was the story shortly. Harry saw one day that her eyes were red, as she passed him, and he would not rest till he had called her into the office and found why; and the why was, that her boy Will had "hooked jack," as the youngster said,— had played truant, and had done it now for many weeks in order, and had done it with the Tidd boys, and the Donegans (sons of perdition as they always seemed), and nothing Bridget could say or do would put Will in any better way. Then was it that Harry sent for the little rascal, "talked to him," she said; but I knew Harry well enough to know what the talking was. He took the boy up country with him one day, when he was making a contract for some wood. He stopped, as they came back, at a trout stream, and bade the little scamp try some of the best hooks from his book. He sent him home, after such a glimpse of a decent boy's pleasures, as nobody ever had shown poor Will before. He sent for him the next day, and told him he wanted him in the office. He dressed the child in new clothes from head to foot. He made him respect himself, in forty ways you or I would never have thought of. Before three weeks were gone, Will was ashamed of his bad handwriting. Before four weeks were gone, he was ashamed of his old company; in a fortnight more, he was the steadiest scholar in the "Commercial College" of the place. Before three months were over, he came to Harry with some lame duck of a Tidd boy whom he had lured out of some quagmire or other. And the upshot of it was, that at this moment Will was as decent a boy as there was in the county; while, but for Harry, he had as fair chance as any of them to be hanged.

That, severely condensed, was Bridget Corcoran's story.

Now, I have no idea of telling how Harry had come to be the star of my worship, — worship which was not idolatry. Talking here at the head of the regiment, how do I know who might overhear me, and this is no story to get into the newspapers. But, while I was reflecting that Harry had rescued poor Will from one set of devils, and me from devils of quite another color, Caroline Leslie looked up. She had joined Bridget and me by the window.

"Do you mean the Caroline Leslie that gives the bird the lump of sugar in Chalon's picture?"

"Why, yes! that same Caroline Leslie. Did you know her?" She looked up. She thanked Bridget very cordially. "I thank you ever so much for telling me that. It has comforted me more than any thing to-day. Will you not come and see me sometime in Worcester? You will find me in 907, Summer Street. Let me write it down for you." So Bridget was pleased. And then Caroline got up and asked me to walk, and took my arm, and we walked the platform together; and she told me what Harry had been to her. How, only three years before, when he first came to Colchester, or to that village, how her brother Edward brought him home, and made her mother say he might board there. How her mother said it was impossible, but consented the moment she saw Harry, when he only came in to tea. How she, Caroline, was a goose and a fool, and a dolt and good-for-nothing, when he moved into that house. And how the mere presence of that man in that family — or was it his books, or was it the people that came to see him? — had changed the whole direction of her life, as an arrow's direction is changed when it glances on the side of a temple. Now, Caroline Leslie was no more in love with Harry than you are. Pretty girl, she had her own lover, and I knew she had. And he, far away across the sea, would shed tears as bitter as hers of that day, when he knew he was never to see Harry's face again.

But we were only three of the Club — Caroline, Bridget, and I. Count Will Corcoran for four if you like. If you count him, the Club is eleven.

But what I tell you will give you an idea. For as soon as we got talking, the bakers and the baked by the stove got talking; all telling much the same kind of story, how dear Harry had been a new life to them. Widdifield, who you would have said had no sentiment, quiet Mrs. Emerson, Mary Merriam, and her brother John, and even Will Morton. I must not try to tell the stories, though I could, every one. We all drew together at last, when something Morton said drew out George Dutton to "state his experience."

"Wadsworth and I," said he, "went out in one of those first California colonies, — when the mutual system was tried in all sorts of ways, and people thought the kingdom of heaven was coming because they all put two hundred dollars apiece into a joint-stock company. On the voyage I did not see him much, and I know I did not like him. How strange that seems now! For there was no reason under heaven why I should not have found him out at the very first moment; and now it seems as if I lost so much in losing all the chance of those five months. Well, I lost it — for better or worse. We came to California, and the colony all broke up into forty thousand pieces. Little enough sticking by each other there! Each man for himself; and, as always happens on that theory, the devil for us all, with a vengeance!

"I roughed through every thing. Got a little dust now and then, and spent it a great deal faster than I got it. I have paid one hundred and eighty-six dollars in gold for a pair of miner's boots,— and they were good boots,— when I had not a rag beside to put upon my feet. At last I thought my lucky time had come. We were up in what they then called the Cottonwood Reach, and a very good company of us had struck some very decent diggings, and had laid off our claims with something like precision, and order, and decency. Wadsworth, as I happened to know, was with some men who had got hold of a water-privilege three or four miles above us. Some of our men had been up to see about buying some water from him, and said he was quite a king in that country. But I had not seen him.

"Then there came in on us, just as we got well established, a lot of roughs, blacklegs, and rowdies, of every nation and color under heaven. They wanted our claims; we all knew that well enough. And they hung round, as such devils as they will, trying all sorts of ways to get a corner of the wedge in. We were a pretty decent set; and none of our boys really liked them, but we were as civil as we could be. Some of the fellows were fools enough to lose dust to them, and I never heard that any of them won any. They pretended to stake off some claims of their own, but they never worked any of any account. They drank their whiskey, and put up tents and shanties for gambling; and swaggered round among the rest of us, and said they knew better ways for washing than we did; and so on. All the time we all knew that something was brewing, while they were about. And sure enough, at last it came.

"Watrous and Flanegan, who were a sort of selectmen to us, had to go down to Agnes City with some gold, and to buy some pork. And they took with them two or three of the best fellows we had. Watrous came to me the last thing, and said, 'Don't you get into a quarrel with these greasers,' for he knew I hated them. But, Mr. Ingham, a saint in heaven would have quarrelled with those men. It all began about a shovel. One of these blackguards came up to me to borrow a shovel, and I let him have it. Then he came back for another, and I let him have that. Then came up three of them and wanted three shovels; and, to make a long story short, we came to words — they and I. They had come up for a fight; and they got it. At last, one of the most noisy of them, — to give him his due, he was half drunk, — drew his revolver and snapped it at me. Lucky for me it missed fire, and in very short metre I hit him over the head with the crow-bar I was using. O, what a howl they made! They dashed at me, and I ran. The first of them tripped and fell; which stopped the others a half second. And then the whole tribe of them, who had been watching the affair, came running after me, yelling and howling like so many wolves."

By this time, as I said, Dutton had the whole group in the station round him.

"Did you ever run for your life?" said he, with a funny twinkle of the eye. "I tell you, — that to put in the best stride you know, and to clear every log, and take no help at any ditch, but just to run, run, run, run, — half a mile, — three quarters, — and a mile, — to feel your heart up in your throat, your lungs pumping, and pumping nothing, — while you just run, run, run, — and know that one false step is death; — I tell you that is what a man remembers. That was the way I ran. I dared not look back. I knew I was well ahead of all but one man. But I could hear his steady step,

step, step, step, — just in the time of mine. Was he taller than I, or shorter? I dared not look round and see. But I knew his stride depended on that. He was gaining nothing on me in time; was he gaining in length of pace?

"Where was I running to? Why, to our poor little shanty, where I had left George Orcutt lame in bed. What safety would that be? These devils could tear it down in thirty seconds. I did not know, but I ran!

"I ran — with the one man close behind, and the others yelling farther back. He did not yell. He saved his breath for running. But he did not catch me. I flung the door open. I crowded down the latch. I stuck a domino from the table in between the latch and the latch-guard, and with this as my poor fortress, I flung myself on the floor. The man dashed up after me, but did not so much as try the door!

"An instant showed why; for in ten seconds the wolves, as they seemed, were howling round him. Then the man, whoever he was, said, 'The first man that steps on this plank is a dead man! There's been enough of this bullying! Dirty Dick, take care you are not seen again in this county. I give you six hours to be gone! Chip and Leathers, you had best go with him, or without him. Your room is better than your company. I will have the sheriff here by night, and we will see what sort of men are going to jump claims on this creek. You fellow with the red beard, who ran away from Angeles, there's a warrant out against you. Understand all of you, that this game is played about through.'

"Who was this celestial visitant? Orcutt and I listened in amazement. Was this the way Raphael addressed the rebellious spirits when Milton was not at hand? Any way, they answered much as the rebellious spirits would have done. Some swore, some laughed, other some, on the outside, turned round and vamosed. So Orcutt told me, whose eye was at a knothole. The celestial visitant said not a word more. But in five minutes the whole crew of them was gone.

"Then I unlatched the door. Raphael came in, and was — Harry Wadsworth! Yes: that light, frail fellow, whom we carried so easily to-day, was the man who looked those beggars in the eye that day, and saved my life for me!

"That was the beginning with me, and there are few things he and I have not done together since that. We have slept under the same blanket, and starved on the same trail. And if any man ever taught me any thing, that dear fellow taught me all of life I know that is worth knowing."

These were the sort of stories we got telling in the station-house, and it was out of such talk that the project of the Club grew. We had not known each other before, but here was one tie we all had together. Could we not then recognize it, by some sort of gathering or correspondence, or union? Natural enough to propose, but you see, of course, what followed.

First, Widdifield — as good a fellow as lives, but set, or as the vernacular says, "sot," in his ways — liked the idea of a Club very much; but thought we must appoint a committee to draw up some little mutual covenant or expression of principles which all the members would willingly agree to. "Something, you know, to give us a little substance." Will Morton did not care so much for any statement of principles, but thought there had better be a constitution made. If he had not changed his coat, he should have had in his pocket the constitution of the Philirenean, which would perhaps have served as a good model. Mary Merriam did not care about any constitution, but thought the society ought to have a name that everybody would understand. Poor Bridget Corcoran did not take in much of all this, but hated clubs. The Shamrock Club, that her husband had belonged to, had worked all his woe. So one thought this, and another said that, and the thing happened, which, so far as I know, always happens, even when ten of the simplest minded people in the world meet together with any common purpose. There has to be a certain fixed amount of talk, — what Haliburton calls the "talkee-talkee stage." It corresponds to the fizz of common air when you open a gas-pipe for the first time. It blows out your match, and you have to wait some little while before any thing arrives that will burn.

One of the Wise Men of the East — was it Louis Agassiz? — said, when he first came here, that one of the amazing things which he found in America was, that no set of men could get together to do any thing, though there were but five of them, unless they first "drew up a constitution." If ten men of botany met in a hotel in Switzerland to hear a paper on the habits of Tellia Guilielmensis, they sat down and heard it. But if nine men of botany here meet to hear a paper read on Shermania Rogeriana, they have to spend the first day, first in a temporary organization, then in appointing a committee to draw a constitution, then in correcting the draft made by them, then in appointing a committee to nominate officers, and then in choosing a president, vice-president, two secretaries, and a treasurer. This takes all the first day. If any of these people are fools enough, or wise enough ("persistent" is the modern word), to come a second time, all will be well, and they will hear about the Shermania.

This was the little delay which killed our little Club at the moment of its birth, if, indeed, it were killed or were born. With regard to that there is a doubt, as you fellows will find out if we should ever get back to this story again.

[At this point, however, the Quarter Master, who had been dying to say something, interrupted Ingham to say it would have been better if the Club had had something to eat, as the organization went forward; and on that, that profane Dalrymple said, "Better something to drink." But Ingham placidly explained that there had never been any thing at the station but doughnuts, and those somewhat tough and musty, and that these had all been eaten by members who had no dinner; that for supper there was nothing left but lozenges, of which the supply was unlimited, but of which man's power of consumption is of nature small.]

So we spent the rest of our five hours discussing the covenant, the name, and the constitution of our little society,— and when at last we heard the scream of the express, and saw its light, we were further from the organization than ever. Everybody looked for scrip and staff (carpet-bag and cane). Everybody seized his coat or his shawl; and poor Widdifield and Morton were just heard pleading for a committee to draw up a constitution, or "just a little formula, you know," when the train stopped, and we stowed away as we could, in the separate cars.

For all that, however, these people loved Harry with their hearts' love; and not one of them meant to fail in the impulse he had given; no, nor ever did fail. And though, as I said, the Club never met again, and never can, perhaps it has existed to as much purpose. After the train was under way, I passed along from car to car, and asked each of them if he would not write me some day, if any thing turned up which brought Harry to his mind, or which would have pleased him.

Everybody said, "Yes." And what is more, everybody has done as he said. So I have this mass of letters you saw in my desk, marked "Harry Wadsworth;" and it is that mass of letters which gives me the material for the really curious story, or stories, I am going to tell you.

If you will come round to my tent after the parade is over, I will show you some of them.

CHAPTER II.

THREE YEARS AFTER.

[*What there was in the Letters.*]

THE fellows did not come up to my tent, regimental headquarters, that night. We were on our way up after the parade, when pop, pop, pop, some red-shirted pickets cracked off their rifles, frightened by some goats I believe; for all this happened in one of the Calabrian Valleys. The companies were filing off to supper as the shots were heard, but halted promptly enough, and, in a minute more, we were all brought back to parade again. I ordered some kettles of polenta brought down for the men to eat, and we lounged and lay there, waiting news and orders for a couple of hours. Then it was clear enough that the whole had been a false alarm, and I let them go to bed.

But a week or two after, Dalrymple, who had made a good deal of fun about the Club, came round, and Frank Chaney with him. Dalrymple knew that I would not have any nonsense about it, and indeed he was quite in earnest himself when he asked me to bring out the papers and tell them more about the Club and its history. I told him what I tell you, that there was no history: there were only these letters, nine of them as it happened, folded together and marked "Harry Wadsworth." An odd-looking set they were. A letter from my wife Polly, written exactly on the third anniversary of Harry's funeral; letters of all sizes and shapes, written on tappa, brown paper, white paper, all sorts of paper; stained, faded, and broken at the edges, but all of them telling of the lives that these nine of the original Club had been leading. Indeed, when we came to look at the dates, they were all written within a month of that same anniversary of the day which we wasted together in the station-house, called *deepo*, at North Colchester.

The letters were: —

A. Dictated by Biddy Corcoran to her son Will, and in the most elegant of clerkly handwriting, down strokes hard and up strokes fine, I assure you.

B. Caroline Leslie's — she had not changed

her name in marrying her cousin Harry, the same who gave her the canary-bird. She wrote from Cronstadt, Maine.

C. George Dutton, written as above, on tappa cloth from one of the Kermadeck Islands, in the South Pacific.

D. Mrs. Merriam,— quiet, every-day letter, from 14 Albion Street, Brooklyn.

E. As above, Polly Ingham's to me, when I was very far off soundings.

F. Widdifield's — he had accepted a place as professor in Clinton College, Kentucky.

G. Will Morton's — he was clerk of court in Ethan County, Vermont; always has been clerk of court, as his father was before him, and as his son will be after him.

H. John Merriam's — book-keeper he, with Pettingill & Fairbanks, Chicago.

I. From Mrs. Emerson — head of a girls' boarding-school in Fernandina, Florida. And I had filed, in the same file, a little paper of memoranda of my own. So there were really the autographs of all, save Mrs. Corcoran, of the ten of the Club which tried vainly to form itself at North Colchester.

Ah! what a pity it is that I may not print all these letters, now and here. If only I, Frederic Ingham, could be the editor of a monthly magazine of my own! If only I had 85,555 readers, on the moderate estimate of five readers to each copy sold, and they were all so prejudiced in favor of the Old as to like to read old letters, and yet so tolerant of the New as to be willing to read my speculations upon them! Then what a title-page could I not make up from these letters alone, for the whole of a number, giving a courteous refusal to all "eminent contributors," and all good assistants not quite so eminent.

To make our "contents on cover:"—
Biddy Corcoran's Home. *By Herself.*
Life by the Furnace.
The Kermadeck Islands.
Housekeeping. *By a Connoisseur.*
Polly to Fred.
Recollections. *Prof. Widdifield.*
Three Years of Life. *W. Morton.*
The West as I saw it. *By a Big Boy.*
A New Boarding-school. *Mrs. Emerson.*
$10 \times 10 = 100$. *Fred. Ingham.*
There, is not that a good title-page for the

outside of your new magazine? Would not that make Mr. Horace's mouth water, as he drew up his advertisement? Would not those running titles be attractive as men opened the uncut pages? If! ah if only I might myself control these MSS. " It must not be, this giddy trance." I must confine myself to the probable restrictions. " Five thousand words, or, at the outside, five thousand five hundred for a single number." These are the hated limits in which I live and move and have my hampered being. Is there not some worthless epithet above which I can strike out? Ah no! better omit all Will Corcoran's commercial college chirography in one lump, and come without preface to pretty Caroline Leslie.

CAROLINE LESLIE'S LETTER. (B.)

It is so queer to see where people will turn up when you least expect it. Now Caroline Leslie, since the funeral, had married her cousin Harry, the same, as I said, who gave her the canary-bird; and he had taken her down to the iron-works at Cronstadt, in Piscataquis County. Pretty girl, how little she thought, when she was giving the canary-bird his sugar, that she was to spend five years of her life in a house just one grade above a log-cabin, with two rooms on the ground floor, and a bed in her parlor, and — which was perhaps the only part of it amiss — that all her friends in Worcester were to be saying that it was "so fortunate" that her husband had such a good position! Good position it was, for all the bed in the parlor. For there Caroline and Harry first subdued the world; there were her first three children born; and there, as the letter showed, she also had done her share of Harry Wadsworth's work, in Harry Wadsworth's way.

When they went down there, it was chaos come again, I can tell you! An old iron-furnace which had been built in the most shiftless and careless way, had made for a year or less some iron of the worst quality, so that the reputation of the ore was all lost, and had then been left to burn out. A new company, with some capital from Ibbotsons or Tubals, or some sort of foreign iron people, had gone in, and had sent down George Landrin, who knew something about making iron, to redeem the reputation of the place, and Harry Leslie to be treasurer and manager as far as George Landrin was not. Instantly, as I need not say, Harry Leslie and Caroline Leslie were married. That was the first link that the new iron company forged, and they forged it without knowing that they did so, by appointing him assistant treasurer, with a salary of fifteen hundred a year. They were married, went to Cronstadt in the first wagon after the roads were in any sort opened, and lived there, thirteen miles from the next town, in a village of iron men; theirs one of three framed houses — all, as I said, one grade above a log-cabin.

"Hajj any ssiety thar?" said Mrs. Grundy to Caroline one day when I met Caroline at her father's, where she had come up to Thanksgiving. How Caroline's eyes snapped and flashed fire! "The best society, Mrs. Grundy, I ever knew." And so it was, indeed, thanks to Leslie, and Landrin, and Harry Wadsworth, and the founder of all good society, the Saviour of all such holes as they found Cronstadt, whose notions in this matter Harry Wadsworth and these fellows had had the wit and heart to follow.

Here is the letter: —

"CRONSTADT, November 7.

"DEAR MRS. INGHAM:

"I have never forgotten that, as we came home from Mr. Wadsworth's funeral, I promised your husband I would some day write to you about him. And though I have put it off so long, I have always meant to do it. But you know how time goes by without our putting pen to paper. It was three years ago that we all met there together. I cannot believe it.

"But to-night I am going to write to you, for I do not know where your husband is, and he must take this as a letter to him. For I have been thinking of Mr. Wadsworth all day. I think of him, and of things he used to say and do, a great deal now we are here in this new life, and I have to try so many experiments, and do so many things for the first time. To-day is Sunday, and on Sundays I see the working-men here even more than I do on other days, and they are more disposed to talk, or perhaps I am. Harry has been gone for nearly a week now, and will not be back till next Saturday, so Mr. Landrin and I and Sarah had to manage about the tunes and singing as we best could last night. But to-day we had stalwart help, and I wish you had been here to see and hear our choir. We still meet for service, as we did when you were here, in the upper carpenter's shop; but yesterday Sarah and Eunice drove the men out just before dark, and began to dress the two chests which make the pulpit with colored leaves, and this morning they completed their decoration, and made quite a brilliant show. Joe Deberry, that French charcoal man who got you the Lycopodium, was very efficient and sympathetic. Mr. Landrin played the flute; Will Wattles read part of a sermon out of the 'Independent;' dear old Mr. Mitchell 'led in prayer,' and we really had a good time — I did, and we all did.

"When we sat round talking, after the service, on the boards and the benches, and a good many outside in the sun, I attacked old Mrs. Follett, and won her heart by asking her how I could dye some yarn I have here. She has always been a little shy of me, but she got talking about this place as it was in the old dynasty.

" It was hell, Mrs. Leslie! I beg your pardon, but it was just hell and nothing else.' And really, I believe it was. When she told me of the drinking and gambling and fighting of men, and fighting of dogs, and of cocks, and of hens and women, I believe, — of every thing really that could fight,— why, Mrs. Ingham, when she told me about what her own husband was, who is now as nice a man as there is in the shop, and what a life she led with him, I wondered whether this were the same world. She thought Mr. Landrin and Harry had done a great deal more than they have. I am sure all we could do here is very little. But Harry has put his foot down, and Mr. Landrin has been very willing to help; and they have said that if they and their wives were here, it should be a decent place to live in; and when I see how happy and pleasant the people are, and when I think how little I used to know about such places and people at all, I thank God for bringing me here.

"All the singers have been up here to-night practising. I wish you knew them all as well as you learned to know Sarah and George Fordyce when you were here. There are some of them who have just that sort of passion for my Harry that your husband has for Harry Wadsworth.

But when they talk to Mr. Leslie about what he has done for the place, he laughs, and points at Harry Wadsworth's picture, and says, 'Don't thank me,— thank him.' Well, to-night ten of them came round to sing, and before we began they produced a beautiful frame for Harry's picture, and asked me to let them put it in, for a surprise to my husband when he comes home. Then they began to talk to me about him, and I told them — well, you know what I told them. And I could see the tears roll down George Fordyce's face as I talked to them. And when they went away, he said, ' We have never known what to call this choir class. I move it be called the Harry Wadsworth Club.' And they all clapped their hands and said it should be so. So after all, you see, your husband's club is born.

"But I must stop. I hear Wally crying in the other room,— and you know I am my own nurse now.

"Give my love to Mr. Ingham when you write. Always, dear Mrs. Ingham,

"Your own,

" Caroline Leslie."

I like that letter; I like that woman; I like that place, Cronstadt; and I like the life they lead there. But I should not have filed that letter, and carried it to Italy and Sicily with me, if the others that came about the same time had not belonged with it; so they all got tied up together. Try this: —

PROF. WIDDIFIELD'S LETTER. (F.)

"CLINTON COLLEGE, BOURBON COUNTY, KENTUCKY, November 10

"REV. F. INGHAM, ETC., ETC.:

"Dear Sir, — In private conversation with a few of our young gentlemen here, I showed to them such of the letters of our dear Mr. Wadsworth as I have with me. They have been very much impressed by their spirit, freshness, and insight into true life. Do you see any impropriety in my printing privately, say a dozen copies for such of these friends of mine as I think might find advantage in them? And should you be disposed to add to them a copy of a letter you once read to me, which Mr.

Wadsworth wrote to you when he entered into
the Polk and Clay canvass so honestly?

"Very truly,

"Your obedient servant,

"INCREASE WIDDIFIELD."

You say those two letters are exactly alike?
Of course; they are all alike. This tappa-cloth
letter is just like that glazed note-paper from
Brooklyn. Want to hear tappa-cloth? It is
not in New Zealandee. Here is the end of
it:—

"It is not true that I am always in scrapes.
You say so, I know; but I do live the steadiest,
stupidest life of any eight-day clock of them all.
Only you do not hear of that. It is only when
I am dragged out of the water by the hair of my
head that I am put in the newspaper, or happen
to mention the incident, and then you all say,
'Dutton is always being dragged out of the
water.' This time it was not metaphorically.

"I had gone off in the *Monarch*, as she took
our six months' collection of *bêche-la-mer*, to see
the last of her officers and to get them well outside the reef, and I had with me my own canoe,

and eight of these native boatmen. They are the best fellows in the world. See if you do not say so before I have done. I bade the Englishmen good-by; they lay to while I jumped down into my boat; and we were off, and I started back for the Cannibal Islands, all my men paddling. Things looked a little grum when we started; there was just the beginning of a nasty Souther, and, to tell the truth, I stayed in the captain's cabin a little later than I meant to. But the men did not mind. I don't think they would mind if they had been in so many cocoanut shells with salt-spoons to bale with. They just stretched to their paddling, begged the after man to see that I was warmly covered, and began chanting this missionary song, —

'Womar iti enata bacha epoku.'

How well I came to know that refrain before I was asleep, and after! For I did fall asleep, and the first thing I knew George caught me by the leg, dragged me awake, and showed me that we had come to the breakers. The sun was down, but it was light enough, what with waves, and phosphorescence, and stars, to make the wildest sight that ever you or I looked upon. Ingham, the thing I thought of was the Cottonwood claims, and my run for my life, and Harry Wadsworth's appearing to the rescue. I knew it would all be over in two minutes. But I spoke cheerily to the men; said, 'All right,' which is one of their favorite words, had that strange feeling come over me, which I dare say you have felt, when one looks death right in the face — the feeling, 'Now I shall know;' nodded to George, who calls himself in their pretty way,

nia-keiki,' which means foster-brother, and said, 'God bless you' to him, and the next second we were under twenty feet of water. Nobody but madmen would have expected to cross that reef with that gale blowing!

"Of course I came to the surface, and of course the curlers swung me over the coral in less than no time! If only they did not swing me upon the next ledge in lesser yet! I could not hold out five minutes in that swirl and spray, and I knew I could not. But before I had time to think much about it, before I had even a chance to clear the water from my eyes to try to see about it, a strong wiry hand had me under the armpit, and I heard George's gentle voice say, 'All right,' and then in their own language he went on to tell me not to be frightened. I was frightened, for the first time, for I thought I knew the faithful fellow could do nothing for me, and I was afraid he would lose his own life trying to save mine. In much fewer words I told him so. But he said just as sweetly as before, 'If I die, you die; and if I live, you live.' And just then I began to see; and near us, in this hollow where we were, between two ridges of breakers, was another of these loving creatures, who said just the same thing, 'If I die, you die; if I live, you live.'

"Ingham, I believe the men saved me by saying that more than by all the wonderful things they did in the next half hour. It seemed to me that it would be so mean if I swamped them or sunk them, that I stuck to my work as I never would or could have done had I been alone. And they — the way they lifted, and pushed, and pulled, — the way they towed me and shoved me, — if we ever meet, you will laugh yourself to death as I tell you, and yet it was no laughing matter then. All eight held together, and held by clumsy, logy me. They understood each other by instinct, and they took me in as they would have taken in an upset canoe if they had found one floating in the offing.

"In half an hour I was lying on the beach here; these loving fellows were chafing me, *lomy-lomying* me, and rubbing oil into me. I could not speak, but I was alive and in this world.

"And what do you suppose was the first thing they did the next morning. I was asleep, as you may imagine, but at sunrise every man of them went off in the offing, which was calm enough now, to hunt up what was left of my boat and to bring her in. And when I scolded George for this, and told him the boat was not worth the risk, he said they knew I loved the boat; they knew I had named the boat 'Harry,' and that my Harry-boat was not to be lost if they could save her. Fred, that was the first time I broke down. I fairly cried at that. And, ever since, they have called themselves the 'Harry-boatmen.'"

You see it is as I said, they are all the same letter, only they are written by different hands, in different inks, on different sorts of paper.

Polly had tied them all up, as they came in, one after another, for six months, and labelled them " Harry Wadsworth," as you saw. Then one day as she went over them, she was tempted to count up the people whom these ten letter-writers told of, as having got clew to our enthusiasm about him.

Here were Caroline Leslie's Harry Wadsworth
    Club 10
Prof. Widdifield's Seniors 12
George Dutton's Harry-boatmen 8
John Merriam's set 7
Mrs. Emerson's "first class" 11
Biddy Corcoran, Will, the Tidd boys and the Tidd
    boys' father and mother 8
Mrs. Merriam's Sewing Club for Newsboys . . . 13
Polly's two children and the two servants, with
    Mrs. Standish 5
Will Morton and the Base-Ball Club at Ethan . . 19
And the men in my own watch, the old quarter-
    master and his son, and the others who messed
    with them, were 9

Polly counted them up. There were 103 in all. But Biddy Corcoran and Will Morton had been counted in the old Club of the station. "There are 101 new members," said Polly. "Ten times ten is a hundred. And it was only three years ago."

CHAPTER III.

TEN TIMES A HUNDRED.

[*An Experience of Dalrymple's.*]

WELL! we subdued the world as we could in Calabria. Then we returned to our respective homes: Garibaldi to his island, I to No. 9 in the Third Range, Frank Chaney to Scrooby, and Dalrymple to that truly English home in Norfolk, which nothing had driven him from but the unrest of an Englishman, — some Io gad-fly, — and the desire of seeing Italy righted, and Vittorio on the throne of Bourbon. In these respective spheres, as assigned to us, we did our part; and I, for mine, embarked in the manufacture of a new sphere and new world, of which no more at present.

Then was it that the parents of Dalrymple urged him to do his duty to the respectable Norman baron who founded his line, and "settle down." Then was it that Dalrymple, seeking for trout in a brook that ran through the ancestral domain, met Mabel Harlakenden, the youngest daughter of a neighboring house. She was sitting on a mossy rock, her feet hidden in ferns, and reading "Coventry Patmore." Dalrymple and she had not met since he broke her father's window with a horse-chestnut on the day of her tenth birthday. Then was it that he introduced himself to her again, and fished no more that day, nor did she read any more. Three months after was it that in the parish church he gave her a ring. The minister took the ring and gave it to Dalrymple, and he then put it on the fourth finger of Mabel Harlakenden's left hand. Then he was taught by the minister. And then they all went home to Dalrymple's father's house to live there.

"Was she a descendant of Mabel Harlakenden of Kent?"

Yes, she was. Why do you interrupt? That has nothing to do with the story, and your question took nine words.

Then Dalrymple proved to be less settled than ever. And it proved that Mabel liked travelling, if it were real travelling, just as much as he. She hated Paris, so did he. He hated

Baden-Baden, — lucky for her, — so did she. He had fished all Norway, so had she. She had hob-nobbed with bandits in Calabria, so had he. Had she ever been to America? — " No, dearest, no!" Would she like to? He had a friend in America, who would put them through, — a man who was with him in Calabria. There was nothing Mabel would like better. So instead of " settling down," as good Mr. Charles Dalrymple had expected, these young people, three months after marriage, took passage in the *Europa*, Captain Leitch, arrived in Boston, stopped at Parker's, took the evening boat to Hallowell, train next day to Skowhegan, and in two days more were laughing and talking at our table at No. 9, in the Third Range.

The prettiest English girl I ever saw was Mabel, — is Mabel, let me say, as she is not here to frown. Dalrymple got his wooden bowl that time. No! I will not describe her. You should have asked him, if you wanted to know. And Mabel and he fished in our brooks, guided by my Alice and Paulina, who in their way were as good fishermen as he.

One night, as we sat together, Dalrymple said,

"Will you show my wife those Wadsworth Papers?"

"Do show them to us, Mr. Ingham," said the pretty girl. "Horace has told me about them once and again, — they were the very first things I knew of you."

Well pleased, I produced the papers, and showed them all I have shown you, and more. Then we fell talking together about Harry, and the Leslies, and Dutton, and all these people; and Polly raked out more letters, which I have not pretended to show you, telling how they had all fared in the three years which had gone by since she tied those nine or ten together. Then Dalrymple asked if, in America, people always shot apart from each other as all of us had done, — here was Harry, born in Maine, to die in Massachusetts; here was I, born in Connecticut, living in Maine; here was Dutton, born in Massachusetts, drowning off the Kermadeck Islands. Was it always so? And I told him the census would tell him that in 1860 there were near seven hundred thousand people in Iowa, where in 1850 there were not two hundred thousand; that the other five hundred thousand were born somewhere; and that the same year there were one hundred and twenty-six thousand people who had been born in Maine, who were living in other States, while only four times that number, men, women, and children who were born in Maine, were living there. I suppose that half the men and women had emigrated. "Happy country," cried Dalrymple, "where no man settles down!"

Then Mabel suggested to him that as they had no plan of travel, as it would be fatal if they should settle down in No. 9, which they seemed likely to do, he could have no better clew to follow in this labyrinth of States than the thread of the very letters he had in his hands. "You love Harry Wadsworth," she said, "as well as any one can who never saw him. I am sure I do." And her great blue eyes were full of tears. "Let us go and see Mrs. Emerson in Brooklyn, — I am sure dear Mrs. Ingham will give me a letter to her; you shall go to Vermont, — is that the name? — and see Mr. Morton; we will both go to Chicago, — which till I heard you speak, Mr. Ingham, I always called Chickago, — and Harry Wadsworth shall introduce us to America."

And so it was ordered. They stayed with us a month longer. I will not tell how many trout they caught, for I should have every cockney scared from the Adirondacks down on No. 9 if I did. But at last the good-byes came, and they started on their way.

No! I shall not write the history of their travels. Little Mrs. Dalrymple may do that herself, and I wish she would. I have only to tell where they crossed Harry Wadsworth's track again.

Dalrymple chose to take boat, instead of rail, west from Buffalo. So they sailed one evening in the *Deerhound*, a famous boat of those days, and their first experience of the floating palace of the western waters. Sunset, twilight, evening of that June day, were as beautiful as hearts could wish, and again and again this young bride and bridegroom congratulated themselves that they had forsworn the train. When bed-time came, Horace led Mabel in from the guards where they had been watching the moon; but before they went to their state-room after midnight, they stopped to watch some euchre-players who were sitting up late in the great saloon.

As they sat there, the captain lounged in. They knew him by sight; he had done the honors at the tea-table. He came up to the table, and said, " Gentlemen, I want you to come forward, and see this schooner on our quarter." Mabel took her husband's arm to go with him; but the captain said, " No, madam, it is too damp for you; we will not keep your husband long," and with the other men walked away.

Horace stayed — how long — one minute or ten — Mabel does not know. But when he came back it was very quickly, and he said in a low tone to the three women who sat together around the deserted table, " The boat is on fire; dress the children, and wake the passengers as quietly as you can. Mabel, wait for me in the after-part of the saloon below this. I will come to you there." And he was gone.

Mabel was probably never so completely her own mistress in her life. She saw that the saloon was as yet uninvaded. She called the sleepy chambermaids, and gave them their messages so calmly that they were not frightened. From state-room to state-room she passed along, and knocked up the sleepers, till her share was done, and well done. Then she went to their own state-room, took the travelling-sack in which Horace had his money and his letters; went downstairs to the after saloon, to wait there as she was bidden.

All this time it was amazing to her that there was so little noise. The engines were stopped. That she noticed. She heard the men at work forward, but forward was far, far away. If she listened, she did not know what were the noises she heard,— plashes; heavy blows as of cutting timber; plashes again,—an occasional sharp word which she did not understand, but around her the still monotone of the saloon, in which there were only herself and two little girls and their mother. And how long this lasted Mabel did not know.

But at last the smoke came. Something— bulkhead or what — I do not know — something gave way forward, and the smoke came, driving, piling right in upon them, so that those hateful lamps which had been so still and clear and unconscious, became, of a sudden, dim spots in fog. The children cried and coughed. Mabel and their mother held them to the open windows.

But this could not last,—the smoke was denser and denser; the women dropped the children out on a pile of cordage that was coiled up in the narrow passage-way behind the cabin, then clambered out of the windows themselves, and in that narrow passage, cramped between the cabin wall and the after-railing, stood alone with the little ones. Then, for the first time, she understood that some freak of the fire had cut her off from the main body of the passengers and from her husband. Or were they four together there, the only persons living out of all? No! somebody was alive forward, for although for a few minutes the air was almost clear, that lasted only for a few minutes;—the fire was gaining forward, and of a sudden the engines began to move again. The other woman said to Mabel, "They are driving her ashore." Whatever was the reason, it seemed fatal to them. The stream of hot air and hot smoke now circled all round them, so that indeed they could scarcely breathe. Mabel looked over the rail, and so did the poor mother. They could see the projecting after timbers and the rudder-head passing through them,—they must do something,—and without a word Mabel climbed down, stayed herself firmly by one of the cross-chains which she found there connecting with the rudder, observed that neither chain nor rudder moved any longer, and then bade the other woman pass her one of the children, and come down herself with the youngest, which she did. How long that lasted, Mabel did not know, — whether it was five miles or five minutes that they rushed over that foaming sea, with that hot air above them, with this slippery foothold below, and her arms growing so tired as she held child and chain. Not so long but she did hold on, however, till of a sudden a sharp explosion forward taught them both that a crisis had come. In a moment more the way of the boat was checked, and in two minutes Mabel saw that all was still, — but the fire. Still that did not drift fiercely back upon them now.

Nobody came near them. Probably nobody could come. But when that horrible weird motion over the foam stopped, Mabel was braver. As for the other woman, she never showed sign of terror from the beginning. Mabel now found she could lower herself enough to sit upon the top of the rudder, and stay herself by a chain above. She did not dare climb up upon the boat again; she then got the child in her arms, and moved out far enough to make room for the other woman. And there, with cinders and smoke flying over their heads, in water to their armpits, holding by rod and chain above them, each with a child embraced,— there those women sat, it must have been for hours. I remember Mabel told me she had to wet the rod above her with the water at last, when the fire from the wreck above heated the rod so that she could not hold it in her hand. She trained the child to splash water up to it so as to keep it cool.

Meanwhile all they could see was flame and smoke in volumes borne high in the air, but away from them, by the gentle wind, as the fire slowly worked its way along to them. All they could hear was the roaring of the flames.

But flames and smoke were borne away from them. The wreck was drifting and drifting nearer and nearer to the Ohio shore. And so in the gray morning the end came. It grounded. Mabel had seen the stars grow pale, it had seemed to her that "the dawning gray would never dapple into day," but it was lighter,—light enough for her to see the shore,—and then one, two, three little boats pushing towards them. And then for the first time these women spoke louder than their breath, and the little children cried aloud again with them. The cry did little, I suppose, but a white handkerchief did more. Swift and straight a flat-boat dashed down to them, a boat-hook struck in the stern-timber above Mabel's head; two men in the bows clutched the two women; and some one cried, "Back her, back her," and they and the two children were safe.

They took them to the kindest, loveliest, poorest home in Ohio, which was just behind the beach. Tender hands undressed those women and children, chafed their swollen arms and hands, rubbed them warm and dry, dressed them in the best the cabin had, laid them on homespun sheets, as clean as they were coarse. And all four slept,—as you never slept.

When Mabel awoke just before nightfall, and tried to make out where she was, wondering at the slabs above her and around her, at the walls papered with Frank Leslie's journal, the only thing her eye lighted on, that she ever saw before, was the portrait of Harry Wadsworth! That was pinned upon the door.

This, then, was what Mabel had taken the ring on her finger for; what she had left her father's house in Norfolk for; what she had started to see the world for! To find herself lying in these coarse homespun sheets, on that queer, high, creaking bedstead; looking Harry Wadsworth's picture in the face; opening her fingers to see if she could open them, after all that clinging to the rod and chain; and trying, by such foolish things as that, to keep herself from asking where Horace was — if he were in this world or in another; where his body was — ah! how wretched — and what she should do? To pretend to drive these questions out of her head, she opened and shut her hands, and wondered if the rust-stains would ever wash off, and looked at her wedding-ring, and remembered the parish church and that winter morning when Horace put it there. It was not in that way that she would forget asking where he was, or if he was in this world or another!

Mabel sat up in the bed. Every thing seemed

terribly still. She looked round the little room. There was not a shoe or stocking on the floor, nor any of her clothes on the one wooden chair.

"Alice!" cried Mabel at last. For "Alice" was the only name she knew of all the people who had surrounded her in these terrible hours. They had called the little girl "baby," though she was four or five years old. The children had called their mother "mother," and "Alice" was the only name that had been spoken.

Alice did not come, but in her place a nice, motherly old lady came, who looked almost as different from anybody Mabel had ever seen before as if she had been one of Dutton's Kermadeck men. But there was the touch of nature there, and Mabel and she were kin.

"Dear child," said the old woman, "cannot you sleep any more? Do you feel at all rested?"

"Have they heard from my husband?" said Mabel, "have any more people been brought in? are there any —— bodies?"

"Bodies? Dear — no, no," said Mrs. Morrow; "do not be troubled about the others; there are plenty of people to take care of them, and they with their own boats too. Do not think about them, dear, and do not cry; let me bring you a cup of tea, and then you shall have your clothes and dress yourself. The men will be back to supper, and we shall know all the news."

"But tell me," said Mabel, "tell me where I am, and where I can write to? What must I do? I never was alone before. I never had to do any thing before — like — like this, you know."

"Like what, my dear lady? — like taking a cup of tea — or like dressing yourself?" And Mrs. Morrow would not stop for an answer. There was a good deal of dry common-sense in Mrs. Morrow, who, after sixty years of emigration, of a new home, of birth, life, and death, of joy and of sorrow, was no longer a fool. She was, therefore, without knowing it, a philosopher. "Come, Amandy-Ann," she cried, bustling back into the kitchen sitting-room, "come, Amandy-Ann, where are you? Here's the English lady awake again, and nigh faint for her tea."

"How did she know that I was an Englishwoman?" said Mabel to herself. She forgot

that if Mrs. Morrow had turned up at the Swaffham station in Norfolk near her father's house,
and had asked her, Mabel, the way to Cockley,
she would have known that Mrs. Morrow was
an American, though she only spoke ten words.
"I must get up and do something," said Mabel
to herself again; "but how can I get up till they
bring me my clothes?"

So they succeeded in keeping her prisoner for
a long hour, while she "worried down" the tea,
and ate a slice of toast, and tried to eat a slice
of corn-bread, which was new to her, and broke
an egg, as Mrs. Morrow had never seen an egg
broken before. When she had pretended to eat
a part of the egg, Mrs. Morrow relented so far
as to let Amanda Ann bring in some dry cloth-
ing, and so to emancipate Mabel from her
prison.

The men came home. An early tea was served
— a meal such as Mabel never saw before. The
men were cheery, though with no grounds intel-
ligible for cheeriness. But they explained that
there were schooners which had run by Huron,
and a certain brig which was known to be beating up to St. Clair, and two freight boats and a

flat which were bound down the lake, and much more than poor Mabel could understand, any of which alone could have rescued all the *Deerhound's* people, if, as no man permitted himself to doubt, they were all in their quarter boats. Indeed, they could rescue themselves. How many hundreds of thousands this cheerful fleet might rescue if it were combined in one, Mabel was too downcast to inquire.

Poor girl! she put this and that together so far as to make out that we, far away in No. 9, in Maine, were the only people in America near enough to her for her to confer with, and she asked Eluathan Morrow eagerly if he could not send a telegram to us from her. Of course he could. He would " hitch up " at once and drive over to Elyria and leave the despatch, so it should go the first thing in the morning. So Mabel wrote : —

I am safe. But I do not know if Horace is. We were in the *Deerhound.*

MABEL DALRYMPLE.

To Frederic Ingham,
    No. 9, in the Third Range, Maine.
By Skowhegan.

Mabel knew enough to know that a telegram must be short. But she was not much used to money yet, poor girl, and she did not know that as the Western Union Telegraph Co. coins it, that despatch cost Elnathan every cent of ready money he had laid up to pay his taxes with the next week. But if he had not had the money, Mrs. Morrow would have sent her three teaspoons to the watch-maker at Elyria rather than have that message delayed. Elnathan rose from table before the rest of them, harnessed up, drove to Elyria, and the next morning the Elyria "Democrat" announced that it stopped the press to say that four more persons had been rescued from the conflagration, a young English lady, and her companion, the mother of two children, who were with her; and that "all these persons were now resting at the mansion-house of our estimable fellow-citizen, Elnathan Morrow, Esq., who has favored us with this information."

After Elnathan had left, poor Mabel did her very best not to be unsociable. Her companion on the wreck was still sleeping off the strain, in the same bed with her two children.

"Do you know," said Mabel, "that the first thing I saw, when I opened my eyes, was the face of a friend? At least I call him a friend."

"Friend?" said Mrs. Morrow, troubled for a moment with the fear that the pretty English girl was wandering. "Who did you see?"

"Oh!" said Mabel, "I only meant I saw his picture — Mr. Wadsworth's picture."

"Did you know Harry Wadsworth?" cried the old lady, and every one else at the table said in the same instant, substantially the same thing.

Mabel explained that she had never seen him herself, and at once, an air of disappointment showed that no one else at the table had ever seen him. But Mabel said to the youngest girl that if she would bring the little travelling-bag which had hung at her side all through the night, she would show her something. So the bag was brought from behind the stove, and Mabel found that the key still turned in the rusted lock. She pulled out a wet handkerchief, rusty scissors, the sloppy, stained bit of canvass work that she had been stitching on the afternoon before — was it yesterday afternoon or was it not sometime in the last century? — and down at the bottom she came to a mother-of-pearl card-case, which had stood the whole, undiluted. Mabel wiped it dry, opened it, looked a moment at another picture which was not stained nor even wet, and from behind that picture pulled out her picture of Harry Wadsworth. It was the last thing that I gave her, except my blessing, when she left us at No. 9.

And then she explained, and they explained. None of them had ever seen Harry in the flesh. But here was Mabel who had seen me, who had seen him, and she had seen letters that he wrote, and if her trunk were ever found, in her portfolio she had a note of his that I had given her. And they — they knew about him. Mrs. Elnathan Morrow — the pale, thin, pretty young woman, the mother of the baby, the one that had said so little, but had been frying the cakes all supper-time, — she came from Ethan, in Vermont. Her brother Samuel was one of the Will Morton Base Ball Club; and she had first met Elnathan, if she would have told the truth, at a reading club at Ethan, where Will Morton read "Monte Cristo" and "Lady Geraldine" to them. And her pale face flushed at last, and her silence thawed, and she did leave the griddle at last and came and sat at the corner of the table, as she warmed up to tell how Will Morton laid down the book one night, and talked to them all about Harry. And of course she told many stories of him, which I cannot repeat here; and then Mabel got to telling some stories that I had told her. And Celia felt as if Mabel and she were old friends, and told her more about Will Morton, and about their life in Ethan, and about the Base Ball Club, and about her brother Sam, who had gone to Minnesota. She told about her own marriage, and how strange it seemed to her to come out here; and Mabel learned that between Ethan in Vermont, and the southern shore of Lake Erie, there was as much difference as between Cockley in Norfolk and Ethan in Vermont; she learned that she was not the only girl that had left her father's house to find a strange, very strange home. If Harry Wadsworth had never done any thing else, he had made sisters of those two women. So they all talked and talked. Just after the June sunset the youngest children slipped in with two great bowls of beautiful strawberries, and Mabel ate from these as she talked, almost unconsciously. The fire in the stove went down, the griddle-cakes grew cold, and it was dark when their long croon was interrupted, as Mrs. Palmer, Mary's companion in misfortune, opened the kitchen door and came in.

Horace? He had been knocked on the head, as he was at work on the forward deck, very early in the business. Some one in the pilot's box hove an axe forward to the mate, who had called for it. Horace was stepping across hastily, the axe struck him in the forehead, knocked him down, and he lay there senseless. The water, leaking from the hose that they were working with, dribbled down on his face sometimes, but nobody could stop to nurse him.

But when the game was played through, when the last quarter boat hauled up under the bow of the *Deerhound*, and the mate for the last time came on board, and said to the captain, " You must come now, sir, there is not a living cat on the vessel," the captain pointed to Horace as he lay there, and said, " Silas, we will heave him down, too. Perhaps there's life in him.

Whether there is or not, it shan't be said that the only two English people in the boat went to the bottom. Handsome fellow he is!" And the captain took Horace by the shoulders, and Silas took him under his hips and carried the senseless body to the opening in the rail; they called two firemen who stood on the thwarts and handed it down, and laid it along as best they could, on the after thwart and in the hollow behind it. Then the boat-hooks shoved her off, and the boat followed the others.

"Them women," said Silas, meditatively, "must have stifled in ten minutes after he sent them there. What on airth made him tell them to go into the ladies' saloon?"

Horace was not killed. Else these pages were not here. The captain never believed he was killed. As soon as the men gave way at the oars, and the boat was well off the wreck, the captain cut off the waist buttons of Horace's clothes, laid bare his breast, untied his neck-cloth, and again and again flung water in his face, as he lay in the arms of that good-natured German, who was wondering, perhaps, if this were the usual mode of travel in America. In fifteen minutes the muscular, full-blooded young Englishman opened his eyes; in three more he was wondering; then he shook himself free, sat up, put his hand to his head, looked round, and began to ask questions.

The burning *Deerhound* could still be seen, and in reply the captain pointed her out to him far astern. Then how boldly the captain lied, as the poor wretch asked after Mabel! You would have thought Mabel was in a Lord Mayor's barge upon the Cydnus, lying upon cushions, fanned by Cupids and rowed by Naiads, so emphatic were the captain's assurances of her comfort and safety, — assurances which Horace was just stupid enough, with the blow, to believe. He grew faint again with his effort, needed a little of the Jamaica the captain gave him, and sank back, with his eyes blurred and his head spinning, on the German's shoulder.

Then it was that the second botch was made in the proceedings of that night. The boats were all pulling for Huron, against a heavy western breeze which was freshening into a gale. The captain's boat was the last of the little squadron, which was pulling in order — it must be near twenty miles—that they might not risk the beaching business with that heavy sea on. By daybreak the others were all safe, and were telegraphed as safe all over the country, while the same telegram reported that the captain's boat was not heard from, and that two women and two children, and an Englishman, name not known, had gone down in the *Deerhound.* This botch all resulted, because, as the captain's boat slowly followed the others, they crossed the line of the little Canadian brig which was beating across the lake back and forth, working her way home from Buffalo to Amherstburg. It was a natural thing, of course, to answer her friendly hail, a very natural thing to run alongside, a natural thing to take the line her skipper threw, a natural thing to go on board, all of them, and to take the boat in tow. Then as towards morning the gale did freshen, and they had to stay on board, it was natural to stay. But because of all this, so natural at every step, when in the fog of the next day she went ashore and bilged on Pelee Island, and they all crawled to land in wet jackets, that was a pity. That was the reason that for four days Horace thought his wife was in heaven; and that for three of those same four days she was more and more sure he was there.

But Horace also fitted off his telegram to No. 9, in the Third Range. And his telegram worked through rather faster than hers, though it started later. The two arrived at Skowhegan the same night. And one express messenger was started for No. 9 in the morning with the two. The weak-minded brother neglected to bring any newspaper with him, so that all that Polly and I knew was in these words: —

We were in the *Deerhound.* Mabel is lost. Address Detroit.   HORACE DALRYMPLE.

And in these, as above, —

I am safe. But I do not know if Horace is. We were in the *Deerhound.*   MABEL DALRYMPLE.

What the *Deerhound* was or where they were, we did not know. But Mabel's despatch was dated Elyria and Horace's was dated London, C. W.; and we knew that C. W. did not mean West Centre of the real London, but Canada West of the — new one.

Poor souls! Lake Erie was between them, — and neither knew if the other were alive.

We gave the boy his supper, fed his horse well, admonished him to bring a newspaper another time, and started him back with the return despatches : —

Your husband is well. Address him at Detroit.

F. INGHAM.

Your wife is well. Find her at Elyria.

F. INGHAM.

And with hopes that they would not go Evangelining and Gabrielling it all over the Western country till they died, we went to bed, still wishing the boy had brought a newspaper, and wondering what had happened to the *Deerhound.*

Mabel got that despatch the third night, so she slept comfortably and happy. Two days still it was before she had any thing but the telegram to live upon; but the telegram was enough, and good Mrs. Morrow's chicken fixings and strawberries and "young Hyson" all helped a little. And they fitted off poor Mrs. Palmer, and little Alice and "baby," for Philadelphia. She thought she might as well go to Philadelphia as anywhere. And at last, five days, I believe, after the night of horrors, Horace came up behind Mabel, as she sat in the piazza with Celia's baby in her arms, put his brown hands on her two cool cheeks, bent over and kissed her, upside down! And Mabel did not faint away!

The next morning Dalrymple wrote to me at considerable length, giving some hint of the story I have been telling, and of his plans for refitting himself and his wife. Here is the end of the letter: —

"While all this goes forward we shall stay here, knowing where we are well off. Poor Mabel really is at home here with these nice people, who are just what you would call clever — as kind as they can be. Do you know, as soon as she opened her eyes, she saw Wadsworth's picture, and it proved that the waves had flung her upon one more of what she calls the Harry Wadsworth homes. And I, — before this poor skipper I tell you of and I had talked five minutes on the logs there on Pelee Island, watching his little vessel as she ground to pieces, I found he was one of Wadsworth's men! What do you think of that? He was a rough customer, but when I said something sympathetic about the loss of the vessel, he answered as cheerfully as a bird, evidently knowing that it was all right. I told him he was a philosopher. 'No,' he said, very simply, handing me back my pipe from which he was lighting his, 'it is not my philosophy, it is my religion. But I don't like to call it so. Our notion is that a man had better not talk much about his religion, certainly had better not think at all about saving his soul. We think he'd better do what he can to save other people's souls, or if he isn't strong that way, save their bodies, or keep them from the devil, some way; and forget he has any soul himself, if he can't do better.'

"Only think, Ingham, of my hearing such words of wisdom out on a fresh-water beach, that did not know enough to have the tide rise. 'Who do you mean by "we"?' I said. 'Oh,' said he, a little nervously this time, 'a little set of us, who don't care to make any noise about our club; we call ourselves Harry Wadsworth's men.'

"Ingham, I started as if I had been shot. Then I was afraid for a minute I was not right in my head, after this dig the axe had given me.

But it was quite clear that the man and the lake and the logs were there, and I questioned him further. He made no secret of it; there were thirty or forty of them who had arranged to get together sometimes, in Detroit, to help each other as well as they could, in their charities, which he represented as mere nothings, but which I found afterwards were what the world's people would make quite a fuss about, mostly among emigrants and sailors. This man, Woodberry, said, as simply as he said every thing else, that it was the only way he had ever experienced religion; that his father and mother were religious people, and he had a brother who was a Baptist minister; but that he did not make much of their notions or their way, but that these Wadsworth people pulled him through a hard turn once when they found him sick in a sailor boarding-house, and he had found since that their religion proved a very good religion for him.

"When we passed through Detroit, he took me round to one of their meetings. It had some of the fuss and form that you and I have seen at lodge, and division, and communication meetings all the world over; but it had a perfectly healthy tone, was true as truth, and tremendously energetic. There was no vow of secrecy, but great unwillingness to get into the newspaper. When I showed my picture of Wadsworth, I became quite a hero. They were glad to hear of the founder of their club from one side more. Remember that, till that moment, I was in the clothes I swam ashore in. What should you say if I told you that it was the President of the Harry Wadsworth Club who introduced me to the Detroit banker who honored the draft on New York, in which I am at this moment dressed, and with which I am shod and hatted. So much for the photograph.

"They have told me of three or four other clubs somewhat like their own. But I do not think there is any effort made to form clubs. It is rather an accident as people drift together. I found they knew all your story of the meeting at the funeral, what you call 'Ten times one is ten.' Some of them were friends of Morton's, some of them had known Professor Widdifield's scholars. They had a printed list of the 'original ten,' as they called them. I showed them Mrs. Ingham's calendar of the one hundred and one people who had had their lives lifted up, and made less selfish in their different ways, as that man's central influence extended. That pleased them; they had not, for instance, known any thing about the Kermadeck Islands, nor what had become of you or Mrs. Emerson. I showed them Mrs. Emerson's letter to me, and told them about my visit to Mrs. Merriam. And then one of the statistical brethren proposed a count, whereat a more godly brother quoted Scripture and explained about David's census. None the less did they count up the people they knew and I knew who this day count Harry Wadsworth as personal friend, personal comforter, adviser, and help to them. Ingham, there were one thousand and twenty-three!

"I will write you again before we leave here. The house has but three rooms, but they make us very comfortable. Mabel needs rest, and has to get clothed again.

"Truly yours, H. D."

I read that letter to Polly, and she said, "Ten times a hundred is a thousand. It was only six years ago."

CHAPTER IV.

TEN TIMES A THOUSAND.

THE Harry Wadsworth Club, which first met in the North Colchester station, had enlarged itself, in six years, without knowing it,—and without trying to enlarge,—to a thousand members. They did not know each other's names,- and there were not many of them who cared to. They had a great many different constitutions. Some were clubs for singing, some were sewing-schools, some were base ball clubs; and this rather formal one at Detroit, upon which, by good luck, Horace Dalrymple had stumbled, had officers,—a president, secretary and records, and all that. All you could say of these thousand people was that, in six years, the life of that young railroad freight-agent had quickened their lives, had made them less selfish, and less worldly. They lived more for each other and for God, because he had lived, and they knew that he had rendered them this service. They showed their knowledge of it in different ways, or some of them perhaps did not speak of it at all. Some of the younger and more demonstrative ones had secret breast-pins with H. W. in a cypher on them. Some of the others, like the Morrows, had Harry's picture framed and hanging on the wall. Some of them, like me, carried it in their hearts, and needed no bit of paper.

But as I say, in six years the ten had multiplied to a thousand by as simple a process as this, —

$10 \times 10 = 100. \quad 100 \times 10 = 1000.$

And, at this fascinating point, alas! I must leave the detail of the story. Indeed, as you see, I have had to leave it already. Of these thousand lives, I have told the story of only four or five, and only a very little part of that. If anybody should tell the story, it would be Horace Dalrymple, who with his pretty Mabel travelled up and down America, backwards and forwards, as the Harry Wadsworth people advised him, sent him, or invited him, for three years and more, after that horrible night on the *Deerhound.*

They saw a great deal of beautiful scenery, and I dare say they " were shown " — as the penny-a-liners love to say — a great many "institutions." They came out in the South Park in the Rocky Mountains; and they went to the Middle Park and to the North Park. I do not know where they did not go. But they did not travel to see "institutions." They did not, in the first instance, go to hunt, or to fish, or to make sketches. They went where one of Harry Wadsworth's men sent them to another. They went from prince to peasant, — you would say, — only there is never a peasant nor a prince west of the Atlantic, nor east of the Pacific. They went from cabin to palace, and from palace to cabin. So they saw what so few travellers see, — the home life of the people here.

These persons they visited did not sit in groups, with their best clothes on, talking about Harry Wadsworth. Not they! A great many of them did not speak his name in a year, maybe did not think of him for a month. "It was not that," said pretty Mabel to me, when she was fresh from this Sinbad life, — "the freemasonry of it was that you found everywhere a cheerful out-look, a perfect determination to relieve suffering, and a certainty that it could be relieved, — a sort of sweetness of disposition, which comes, I think, from the habit of looking across the line, as if death were little or nothing; and with that, perhaps, a disposition to be social, to meet people more than half way."

Thus spoke the little Englishwoman; and I, in my analytical way, used to the inevitable three heads of the sermon, said to myself, — "Humph, that is Mabel's translation of faith, hope, and love."

Horace and Mabel, after their three years' journey, had found us living in South Boston. We were sitting after dinner one day on the wood-shed behind the house, which served us as a piazza, when Horace laid down his pipe, and asked me if I remembered explaining to him the way in which people dispersed over the United States, — so that the census shows that each State is made up from the children of all. I had forgotten it, but he recalled it to me.

"That was what first set me on this journey," said he, "which has carried us so far. Now the queer thing about it is, that it is no special law of your country, this dispersion and radiation; it is a law of all modern civilization."

"Of course it is," said I.

"Of course it is," said he. "Here is this Connecticut pinmaker." And he took out from his pocket-book a bit of green paper, evidently torn from a paper of pins, on which the man said that he was "pinmaker for the people of the United States, and for exportation to all parts of the world." "Now, that," said Horace, "is what you call a piece of buncombe; but, for all that, it is true. The old statement is true, that if you import into Russia a bottle of champagne or a piece of broadcloth, you import liberal ideas there as truly as if you imported Tom Paine. Commerce is no missionary to carry more or better than you have at home. But what you have at home, be it gospel or be it drunkenness, commerce carries the world over. As what's-his-name said, the walking-beam of Livingstone's steam-launch preached as well as Livingstone, and a good many more people heard it."

"It would not have said much if Livingstone had not been there," said I, a little crustily.

"Don't be sore, padre," said Horace. "Nobody said it would. But you see Livingstone was there. That is just what I am saying. And there are Livingstones all over this world, who are not acquainted with the Royal Geographical Society. As we came on from New York last night, after Mabel turned in, I got out this note-book, and I added up the number of men and women who belong to these different Wadsworth clubs, who have travelled or settled in different parts of this world. Just look at them."

Sure enough I found Horace, — who was always a better acting adjutant than he was any thing else, — true to his nature, had entered in close columns, forty lines to a page, the people that any of the Harry Wadsworth people regarded as being really in earnest in relieving the suffering of the world, and getting the world out of the mud. " There's a sort of law of average about it," said Harry. " Every now and then a member dies. Then I make a red star, — so, against him. But, on the average, you find that every working man, or especially every working woman in one of these lodges, or clubs, or singing-schools, is represented at the end of three years' time by ten persons whom he has started on a better kind of life than he was leading before. When I was with these people at Detroit, after I got my head knocked open, we counted up a little more than a thousand, of what they called, in their stately way, 'affiliated members.' Your wife, here, was one of their 'affiliated members.' But I have got here, now, — in three years' more time, — see here," — and he turned over page after page of his crowded note-book. At the end was a rough count — 10,140. "That is what three years have made of one thousand and twenty-three, so far as we know. Of course, a great many of them are wholly out of our sight."

Little Pauline, who is an enthusiast about Harry Wadsworth, though she never saw him, clapped her hands with delight, as Horace said this, and cried out, "TEN TIMES ONE THOUSAND IS TEN THOUSAND."

"Do you learn that at the Lincoln School?" said Horace, with approval. "I shall have to put you on my register, I believe. But what I was saying, Ingham, is this: Here are underlined with blue all the seafaring men in this list. See how many. With red are all the Englishmen,

Scotchmen, Germans, and the rest, whose homes are likely to be in any part of Europe, — see here, and here. With green are marked the Asiatics: people at Calcutta, — there's a man at Singapore, — all these are Japanese men. And these, underscored with black, — there are fifty-one even of them, — are in Africa; you would say it was impossible. But what with Algiers, Alexandria, Zanzibar, the Cape, and a good many men and women who went to Liberia, Harry Wadsworth and his loving life are represented, so far as that, in Africa."

Then Horace went on to say, that for himself his travelling was over. The people at home were wild to see Mabel and her baby. The child himself was weaned, and he should finally " settle down " with the two. " I can do as much at home in renewing this world, and bringing in the kingdom," said he, " as if the Arapahoes were scalping me. And I foresee that my mission ground is Norfolk, which I did not suspect when you and I were in Calabria. What I have to say now is this, that in Norfolk I shall constitute myself the assistant adjutant, for that quarter of the world, of these Wadsworth people. I mean to keep up the list of these whom I have marked with red. If I write one letter every morning and one every evening to them, and four every Sunday, I can write in three years twenty-five hundred letters to one part of Europe and to another. I mean to find out, before three years are over, what the radiating influence of one Christian life is, in a quarter of the world which the man never saw who lived that life."

We were talking this over, when we met the others at tea. Mabel was full of it. She really knew the Coffins who had gone to Sweden and the Wentworths who were at Dresden, and I know not how many more she meant to write letters to, and get information. Mary Throop was taking tea with us. One of the real steady-going people she, capable of immense enthusiasm, all the more, because she never shows any, — no; though you put her on the rack and pull her tendons asunder, — the approved way of awaking enthusiasm. She looked over Dalrymple's book with approbation, nodded silently once and again, understood it all the better because no one explained it to her, smiled her approval as she gave it back, and said, "I am going to get a book. I am going to take Asia."

"Will you?" cried Horace, exultant. "I had not supposed anybody else would care any thing about doing it. But if you only will! You see, my dear Miss Mary, it is not the glorifying of this young man, that is the last thing anybody wants to do. It is that any life as noble as his and as pure as his never dies; and that his power to lift up the world is always going on!"

Yes: Mary Throop saw that too. She had not enlisted herself for any work of mutual admiration. She wanted to register the real diffusive power of right and truth and love and life. She would do her share.

Horace thought a moment and said, "If you really will take Asia, I know who will take Africa. Mabel, do you not remember that great black man on the railroad from Memphis? Here is his name, Fergus Jamiesson. He will take Africa. He had been up the Niger. He had a passion for statistics. And I have his card somewhere. We can have the whole world. For there is nothing the Detroit men will like better than to keep up America. I will write to-night to Taylor and to Wagner. They have the statistical passion there also."

"For my part," said Polly, "I detest writing letters to people I never saw. I believe you men like it, because you did it in the army,— and you thought King Bomba was beaten when you had emptied a pigeon-hole by putting all the papers into big envelopes, and writing on the outside 'Respectfully referred to Major Pendennis.'

"For my part," continued she, "I had rather the children should spend their money on a grab-bag at a fair, than bring me home a parcel of letters from the fair post-office, that were written at a venture, from somebody to nobody, to be posted nowhere, because they were good for nothing."

Mabel laughed and said, "Amen, amen. But you see, dear Polly," said she, "or you shall see, that these letters of ours are written by somebody of flesh and blood, to somebody of blood and flesh, with something in them and going — to Sweden, — mine are."

"Humph," said Polly incredulously, "they will take the express train back to Weeden station when they get there." But Mabel only laughed the louder, said she should write her first letter then and there; that Mary Throop should write hers and that Horace should write his.

"And Polly," said I, "shall pay the postage, out of our rag-money."

So the three first letters in this gigantic correspondence were written that night in our sitting-room in D Street. They were read, criticised, postscripts added, and then forwarded; and so the second half of the formation of the Club began.

CHAPTER V.

EUROPE, ASIA, AFRICA, AND THE ISLES OF THE OCEAN.

YES, it is true that the next three years of this history become a little less determinate. There is less of that "realism," as the critics call it,—which the critics so much dislike, because it makes you sure that what you read is true, instead of being bookish, and in general improbable or unreal, as the critics think all truly good writing should be. You see it was on the 24th of March, 1870, that Dalrymple and his pretty wife left our house to take the *City of Brussels* for Queenstown and Liverpool,—and from that day to this day I have never seen their faces more. Also Mary Throop has never been in D Street again. As for Fergus Jamiesson, I never saw him, far less the Detroit corresponding secretaries. What I am now to tell, therefore, of the three years between 1870 and 1873, I am to compile from statistics, files of letters, and the law of general averages; and it will have much more the vague air of ordinary history, therefore, than the truth truly told ever does,—from which, as you know, ordinary history is indefinitely removed.

Sparing you the detail, then, in which prophecy and history fail alike, here is the sum of the story. Of the TEN THOUSAND Dalrymple had the names of I know not how many hundreds of men and women, who from this cosmopolitan country of ours had carried Harry Wadsworth's name or his picture, or his printed letters, to one or another part of Europe, or if not these, had carried the spirit of his life there. They had what the Detroit men called the four cornerstones,— and in Detroit had painted on four slabs in their lodge-house: "They "looked up and not down," "they did not talk of themselves," "they always lent a hand," and "they were not afraid to die." Yes, and they knew, but for Harry Wadsworth, they would have thought more of themselves, would have been brooding and regretting,— would have been slower to help,— and would have clung tighter to life.

With these eight hundred, more or less, men and women, Horace and Mabel began their correspondence: three letters a day, counting hers, and five or six every Sunday. Well for them that postage was coming lower,— but they sold their foreign stamps for the benefit of the cause. That was an economy Mrs. Haliburton taught them.

Well! a great many letters never were answered, perhaps a third part. But on the other hand, it proved at once that there were in Europe already many more of the apostles, as Dalrymple began to call them, than he and Mabel had any idea of. They had to open new books, with much wider margins, and much more space between the lines. Iron-men had not been ironing in Sweden without carrying there the old Cronstadt lore; railroad men did not go to Russia without carrying there the North Colchester traditions; young artists did not paint in Rome without talking to their model boys, brigands or beggars, as it might happen, in the spirit with which Harry talked to Will Corcoran and the Tidd boys. Nay, Horace even went down into Calabria and established an order there among people as black as the most veritable Carbonari; and he was fond of saying that he found there some Italians, who remembered the padre Colonel Ingham, and who had not forgotten what I had told them, in my wretched way, of Harry.

I think Mabel was most touched, when, as they were coming home through Thuringia, and had stopped on her account for a day or two, at the smallest and least pretentious inn that ever escaped from being put into Murray, the tidy girl who fried the trout, made the bread, smoothed the pillows, brushed away the flies, and in the evening played on the guitar, — proved to speak English, and proved to have learned it at Manitowoc, in Wisconsin. Mabel was so far Westernised by this time, that she clave to the German girl as to a sister, — more, I am afraid, for the flesh is weak, than if the girl had been a bar-maid in Norwich or in Aylsham, rather nearer Mabel's home than Manitowoc was. Be this as it may, they sisterized at once. Mabel talked Wisconsin to her, and she talked of the Lakes to Mabel, — broken English and broken German got cemented together; and before they were done, the Fraulein had produced a Harry-Wadsworth breast-pin! They had had a little church there in Wisconsin, back twenty miles from the lake, where one of Widdifield's men was the minister! And this girl also had learned "to look forward and not backward, to look up and not down, to look out and not in," and to "lend a hand." And when she came back to Thuringia, in the little guest-house there, she had organized a chorus of peasant-girls, who met her once a week, and read their Bibles together, and sung together, and knitted together, and four times a year gave away the stockings they knit to the old women in the charcoal huts, — the witches of seven generations ago, — and they did this in memory of Harry! So far that little candle threw its beams! They showed her the copy of "Frank Leslie," which had the picture of the dedication of the Wadsworth Library Hall in Pioneer, Missouri.

But I said I would not run into detail. Nor will I even cumber the page by the nicely ruled table Dalrymple made up for me three years after he left us. I had enough rather copy scraps from Mabel's crossed letters. She wrote freely to us, and did not count those letters among the official ones. But I will not do that. Nor will I ask you to follow Mary Throop through the mazes of her Asiatic correspondence. Queer stamps she got, with her Singapore mails, and her Assam distribution offices, — and Galle and Shanghae and Petropaulowsky, and End-of-the-earth in general. Nor will I offend the proprieties by copying the very indifferent spelling of Fergus Jamiesson, writing from Monrovia, — nor explain the great difficulties of his inland correspondence. Far less will I try to condense within these waning pages the full and triumphant statistics compiled by the recording and corresponding secretaries, and the staffs of assistant correspondents and assistant recorders of the Detroit central " Office of Registration." Do not we all remember George Canning's words? "I can prove any thing by statistics, — except the truth." So we will let the statistics go, accepting only the results.

For, about the time I got Dalrymple's elaborate letter of his three years' observation in Europe, Jamiesson's from Monrovia came. Before long, there appeared an immense printed document from Detroit, and then we wrote to

Mary for her Asiatic statistics. Queer enough, the old law held! In three years, everybody who cared for this dissemination, by personal love and personal work, of the spirit of an unselfish life, had found some nine, ten, or eleven people like himself. The average ran at ten, as it had done.* And when Pauline, who was now a big child, added up all the columns, they came out, under this eternal law, **107,413**. "TEN TIMES TEN THOUSAND IS A HUNDRED THOUSAND!" That was the one remark which Pauline volunteered on the occasion.

CHAPTER VI.

TEN TIMES A HUNDRED THOUSAND.

AND so my story is well-nigh done. Not because there is no more to tell, but because there is so much to tell. Anybody can count the seed-leaves on an elm-tree the year it starts, but Dr. Gray and Mr. Peirce are the only people I ever heard of who computed the leaves on the Washington Elm; and the man to whom they told the sum forgot whether there were a million or ten million, because neither the word million nor the words ten million gave him much idea or meaning. I could tell you how Harry Wadsworth made the first ten what they were, but I could only hint of the way the first ten helped the first hundred. I could only pick out one story of the work of the first hundred, and of the first thousand I know I have told you nothing. But nothing dies which deserves to live. Fifteen years after he was dead, we loved him all the same; and every true word he spoke went over the world with all the same power, though it did happen to be spoken in the language of the Ngambes by a chief of the Barotse to a woman of Sesheke. Wildfire does not stop of itself; and when a hundred thousand blades of grass are really on fire, it does not stop easily. So the next three years from this count of Pauline's proved.

Dalrymple had also had to appoint secretaries for France, Southern Italy, Northern Italy, and the rest. His polyglot was not very good, and he said different nations had different ways. So it was in Jamiesson's continent also, Kilimane and Sesheke, Ossuan and Jinga, there were many languages, many methods, little writing, and no mails. But love worked wonders easily in that African blood, and Jamiesson had most extraordinary stories from traders, and cameldrivers, and boatmen, and ivory carriers, and I know not whom. In Asia they got things going with their own Asiatic fervor, and they went forward with a rush when they were started. All religions have begun there, and our co-operation in true life, which was no new religion, but only a little additional vigor with a little more simplicity in the old, was at home on the old soil. And here in America, I need not tell how many forms of organization and of refusal to organize, how many statements, platforms, movements, combinations, head centres, middle centres, and centre centres, would develop in three years.

What pleased me in it all was this,—that nobody, so far as I could find out, got swept away with the folly of counting noses. Nobody seemed to think he was subduing the world,— because he was in a correspondence bureau and kept count of those who subdued. I do not believe anybody gave more time to the correspondence than Horace did,—a letter before breakfast, and another as he went to bed,—perhaps half an hour a day. On the other hand, I am perfectly sure that Horace was ten times a man, because he was thus thrown into outside relations. What does the third "plank" say, but "Look out rather than in." It was near the end of these three years that they made an attack on us, Horace and Mabel, and insisted that our four oldest girls should make them a visit. We said it was nonsense,— but the girls did not think so,— and after many obstacles set up by me, Horace and Mabel and the four girls conquered; and, trampling over my body, Alice, Bertha, Clara, and Pauline, all sailed for England, went to Norfolk, and made a most lovely summer visit there. Horace took them up into Scotland, and they tried salmon-fishing there,— all of them, Mabel and all, went to the Lakes together, and they slopped with their water-colors there; but the very best of all was at home. That was so homelike, so English, and so lovely. I think Mabel's father, in his heart of hearts, thought that these four girls were the most extraordinary things which Horace had ever sent home from his wanderings; that no stuffed kangaroo, or no living emu of his boyhood, equalled these four adventurous living specimens. But none the less did he come over daily to the house to see what could be done that day for their amusement. And Horace's own father, as the girls by one accord declared, was "just lovely."

Of which visit, let them write the history,— in this place only this is to be noted: that excepting when Pauline went bodily into Horace's den, and compelled him to show her Wadsworth letters, they hardly saw or heard any thing of the secretary's duties as secretary. What they did see was the eager, cheerful life of a conscientious gentleman in the midst of a large tenantry. They saw farms in perfect order; they saw laborers with the lines of promotion open; they went into schools of cheerful, bright, intelligent children, well taught and thriving; they saw all the time that Horace was lifting where he stood; and that by Swaffham in Norfolk, he was driving out the King Bombas of that region quite as effectually as he drove out another King Bomba from Calabria. His vocation was that of an English land-proprietor, compelling deserts to blossom and bear fruit; his avocation was so near to it, that it was hard to discriminate. It was the making the men who worked on his estates to be more manly, and the lifting up their children's lives; yes, and without their knowing it also, the farmers who only paid him rent, and the laborers whom they hired, and their children also, were lifted up in the general renovation. These were the vocation and the avocation. For a little "Third," as he called it, — a pastime of his dressing-room, — he kept up the correspondence with such Englishmen as believed in the four cardinal points, and were trying to make other people live by them.

Norfolk, Norfolk, Norfolk, — always Norfolk, with its dear English names, Swaffham and Cockley and Aylsham, and I know not where not, — are the burden of the girls' tales of this celebrated English visit. But the end of it is the part which specially belongs in this history of mine; namely, the expedition they all made to Baden-Baden. A queer place, you would have said, for Horace and Mabel actually to start for, having no other object than to entertain four country cousins, — that is, my four girls. But you say this because you do not know that the Prime Minister, and indeed half the government, and the Crown Prince himself, were, at this time, all enthusiasts for "the four cardinal points" named above; and had, long before, painted these statements of them, in letters of gold on the four sides of the Kursaal, where you, Mr. Chips, remember losing five hundred rouleaux the night before you left for home: "Sursum

corda," "vorwärts nicht ruckwärts," "αὐτούς οὐ
σαυτόν," and "lend a hand." This was the way
they rendered the four legends, which Detroit
had been satisfied to print in our vernacular. I
need not say that the whole gambling business
was at an end; but though they were virtuous,
there were cakes still, and what took the place
of ale. The government — younger men than
you and I remember in Baden — were all of them
enthusiasts, and all of them æsthetic. They
declared that they would show that Baden-Baden
without high play could be made more attractive
than Baden-Baden with it: they gave the four
"cardinal points" for the secrets of the attraction,
and certainly they succeeded. The drama of
Weimar was never better than theirs; the out-
door life of Baden-Baden itself, in its tawdry
days, was never as luxurious as this was now;
the fine art of Munich was more grandiose, but
not half so lovely as this; and, what with pretty
girls, enthusiastic artists, an opera beyond re-
proach, the perfection of comedy, the most
agreeable men in Europe and the most attractive
women, — the people who came there managed
to live without *rouge et noir*, — at least my girls
did.

But they did not go there for mere agreeable living. It was, as we know, rather more than eighteen years since that meeting of ten of us, in the North Colchester station house. It was three years since, as I told you, Pauline added up her "hundred thousand" of the multiples of that original ten. And at the end of the eighteen years, the Crown Prince had determined to call together privately a Conferenz of corresponding secretaries; not, as he said in his circular, for the purpose of making any plans, — for, as he supposed, the great merit of our movement was that it never had any plans, — but that the secretaries might know each other by sight, and, at least, have the satisfaction of shaking hands. "If they did nothing else," said the Crown Prince, "they could show each other how they kept their record-books." So they assembled, — and for four of Horace's suite I can testify that, as we say down East, "they had an excellent time." But it was the queerest assembly that ever came together in that Kursaal.

Sailors from the Levantine ports, old long-robed men from Poland, who looked like Shylock, but were very unlike him, cloth-men from the depths of Germany, quiet Spanish scholars from the university cities, two quaint-looking schoolmasters from Holland, and nice stout men, who, Alice is sure, were burgomasters. Then among all this white trash, you might see Jamiesson himself, great quiet black man, a little overdressed, and his crew of all colors, camel-drivers, pottery-men, wool merchants, cadis, and muftis. Mary Throop was there, looking in the face, for the first time, beys and effendis, with whose autographs she had been long acquainted, and talking, with smiles and with gestures, to people who spoke " Central Tartary " and " Turkey-in-Asia," but of other lingo knew none. All, save a herd of black-coated Americans, looked like a fancy ball, as Clara said, of a thousand people who still moved about as if they had all breakfasted together and were entirely confident in each other, and were never to part from each other again. At the first meeting, two or three hundred out of the thousand had each his recordbook under his arm; and, on the old faded green of the tables, left in memoriam, you would see a Spaniard trying to explain to a Pole about his totals, his gratifying coincidences, and his surprises, — holding up his fingers by way of count, and the Pole bowing, and sympathizing, and saying, " Ah!" and "aussi," under the impression that "aussi" was Spanish for "yes." It was very funny to the eye, — for it was the Tower of Babel backwards. It was all languages and peoples united again under the empire of love.

No! They would not have any meeting for speech-making, lest they should get into the old ruts. Only, on the day fixed for the first assembling, the Crown Prince made one very satisfactory speech, with occasional quotations of the four mottoes, pointing to them, which was cheered loudly by those who did not understand it, and equally loudly by those that did. Then, instead of the usual forlornity of a convention, they all fell to talking together, and a charming buzz arose. Dark-eyed secretaries from Bulgaria were seen talking to blonde secretaries with curls from the neighborhood of Fort Scott, in Kansas; a very business-like secretary from Oshkosh was caught talking, behind a door, with a very pretty Circassian secretary who had brought her book all the way from Himry. The result of a week's rapid talking, with drives, and walks, and concerts, and picnics, was very great mutual confidence and regard among the secretaries, more, as Pauline thought, and as Mabel agreed, than if they had all sat on uncomfortable settees eight hours a day for a week, and had discussed some resolutions that nobody cared a very great deal for. Only then there would have been so much more to put in the newspapers! And what is life good for, if you cannot put it into the newspapers?

Meanwhile, the secretary of state was at work with a detail of clerks furnished him by the home department; and the different secretaries brought in their books to him, and their totals were transcribed and added, and put into all sorts of tables, in the most admirable way, so as to look quite as dull as, in reality, the miracles they described were exciting. And the result of the whole was, that in the three last years the movement had gained TENFOLD! Each individual member seemed, on the average, to have brought in ten new members, or so nearly ten, that the deaths in three years were made good, with nine members more. The grand total increased the 107,413 members of three years before to 1,081,729! So soon as this was proved, a royal salute was fired from the old batteries. And, that evening, the court-band performed for the first time a magnificent new symphony, by the great Rudolphssen himself, of which the theme was *Zehn Mal Eins ist Zehn*, which was received with rapture by all who at all appreciated classical music. I am sorry to say some of the Chinese secretaries did not. But as there was not room for them to sit down, they walked in the gardens in the moonlight. Of all which glories Bertha wrote full accounts to us, winding up, in immense letters, with what was everybody's motto and badge at Baden-Baden,—

TEN TIMES A HUNDRED THOUSAND IS A MILLION.

CHAPTER VII.

THE CONFERENZ AT CHRISTMAS ISLAND.

AND so after a little of Switzerland, and a dash at Rome and at Naples, my girls came home. No: no matter what secretaries they had met, that is not part of the story. It had certainly been the most curious convention that ever was held; with no speeches except this by the Crown Prince, and, instead of Resolutions, nothing but a Symphony. A convention which ended in a symphony! Nothing but a symphony! As I heard Kate — who had been to Trinity for she knew what — say, bitterly disappointed, that there was "nothing but prayers" there; — and as the pretty Baroness Thompson when she returned from her wedding-tour, — when they had arrived at Niagara too late for the hops at the hotels, — told me that there was nothing at Niagara but water! A convention with nothing but a symphony! But not so bad a convention after all.

For it sent all these secretaries home well convinced that there was much more in the movement than figures; and that they and the cause they loved were lost if it were shipwrecked on statistics;—that dear Harry Wadsworth himself would be dissatisfied, even in heaven, if he thought one of them was getting betrayed into preferring a method to the reality. " Love is the whole," said the Piscataquis Secretary to me, as he stopped at No. 9, with some letters from the girls;—and I know he went down to his camp of lumbermen more resolved than ever to lend a hand,—and some very noble things we heard from that lumber camp before the next year had gone by.

But I have forsworn detail. You see we are rushing to the end! From this great Conferenz the story of the movement is indeed mixed up with the larger history of the world. It was only then that for the first time many in the movement, and many out of it, knew that there was any movement at all. A stone is thrown into the water, but who ever knows where or if the sixth circle strikes the meadow-grass on the shore?

Nor did we hear of any Conferenz or Convention three years after, till it was too late for us. We went on in our quiet way. Life was purer and simpler and less annoyed to us, because constantly, now, we met with near and dear friends whom we had not known a day before, and who looked up and not down, looked out and not in, looked forward and not backward, and were ready to lend a hand. Life seemed simpler to them, and it is my belief that, to all of us, in proportion as we bothered less about cultivating ourselves, and were willing to spend and be spent for that without us, above us, and before us, life became infinite and this world became heaven.

But there was a Conferenz, though we did not know of it beforehand;—without taking down the dictionary I cannot tell what they called it. It was in one of the South-Sea Islands, set a-going by some of George Dutton's Kermadeck people. They could not go to Baden-Baden, of course; and I believe the whole Pacific Ocean had had but two representatives there. Their canoes could not double Cape Horn, they said. But when they heard the accounts of

Baden-Baden, they all said that, for all its glories, it was still true, — as Mr. Morris had made out, — that the earthly paradise was in their own beautiful ocean, — Pacific Ocean indeed, if any one understood the sublime prophecy in which it was named. So the Bêche-la-mer people, and the seal-fishers, and the Nootka Sounders, and the birds'-nest men, and all sorts of Alexander Selkirks, and Swiss Families, and Peter Wilkinses, and Crusoes without a name, — all the Judds and Bishop Selwyns and Pitcairns Islanders fell to corresponding with each other, and organized their own celebration of the seventh triennial anniversary of the original club meeting. It was to be held on Christmas Island, for the name was of good omen; and, as near as they could figure, that was near the centre of the Pacific, and on the whole equally convenient and inconvenient to everybody, — like a well-placed school-house in the school district of a country town. Great correspondence they had with other secretaries, and great temptations they offered of bread-fruit and poe, and cocoa-nuts, and bananas, with actually unlimited supplies of guava jelly, to any who were carnally minded, if they would come. Great efforts they made to get some of the "original ten," and with such success that the Widow Corcoran went, and one of the Tidd boys, and Widdifield,— and great heroes, I can tell you, they were too. And in every sort of craft the ocean bears did the delegates from different groups arrive; from groups with names, and groups without them. As by those ocean currents the original cocoanuts were borne wafted in their husky boats; and every seed and every egg that has been needed since for the food of man or beast,— so the delegates or secretaries came north, came south, came east, and came west, to Christmas Island. And they held high festival there for many days. George Dutton was there, evidently no day older than he was when in California he ran for his life. Widdifield met college pupils of his, whom he had not seen since he preached in Newark in New Jersey. Mrs. Corcoran met some people from the Old Country who had been living in Honolulu for twenty years; but on conversation it proved that from their old home in Ballykeir they could see Stevie's Mount in the sunrise, which she,

Mrs. Corcoran, always saw in the sunset, when, as a little girl, she came and went in Ballytullah; and, though neither of them had ever gone to Stevie's Mount, by going round the world, they had met here on Easter day on Christmas Island. Strong representations from Japan were there, of those charming, mild-spoken, gentlemanly noblemen, and in the ardor of the movement some of them had ventured to bring their sisters and their wives.

And there, too, they had their symphonies in their own kind, — though not after the fashion of the court-band of Carlsruhe. Symphonies in dancing, symphonies in canoes on still water behind guardian reefs, symphonies whispered in the ear, symphonies spoken in prayer to God by great congregations; — there was no want of symphonies, and no want of harmony, though there was not a resolution or programme or preamble printed or voted for, nor so much as a cornet-à-piston on the whole Island. The secretaries had their books, tappa books and books of rice paper, books of cotton, books of sealskin, books from America ruled by Leveridge and Stratton's compound, patent, self-adjusting, double combination ruling machine, and long rolls of parchment which some Muftis brought from beyond Muscat. And speculative secretaries and calculating secretaries lay for days with their books under fronds of giant ferns, twenty feet high, — yes, just as lovingly as the fairies lie under the maiden's-hair in the spring pasture, — and calculated and copied, subtracted, transferred, cancelled, and added. Immense correspondence they opened from absent secretaries, and then calculated more, made more transfers, and added more. Then they filed the letters, and went off to their dancing, or talking, or story-telling. Then the next day they met and calculated again, and more boats and ships brought more letters. And after two or three weeks the whole was put in the proper tables, and the great law, "Ten Times One is Ten," was verified again. In only three years from the Conferenz at Baden-Baden it was made certain that the movement was represented by at least 10,934,127 members. There was immense jollification at the announcement, — a great international feast of two finger and three finger poe, with roast-beef, bêche-la-mer, birds' nests, and guava jelly, *ad libitum.*

And when all had well feasted, George sent off his own lovely clipper yacht, the " Harry Wadsworth," which had long before taken the place of the shattered canoe, with a skipper who cracked on day and night to Hawaii, and telegraphed to the four continental secretaries only these words : " Ten million nine hundred and thirty-four thousand, one hundred and twenty-seven." " Only these and nothing more." And the next morning, all over the world where there were newspapers, in the head line of the " Personal " in the leading journals of the towns where were secretaries, there appeared in full-face italic capitals these words only, understood by the elect, if by no others : —

TEN TIMES A MILLION IS TEN MILLION.

That was the way in which the Christmas Island meeting and its results were first announced to me and to Polly. We had been at No. 9 for four or five months, and by misfortune all our letters from the Kermadeck Islands had gone to D Street in Washington, because the Kermadeckers had neglected to put " South Boston " on them. Then they had been sent back from the dead-letter office to the Island; and when Dutton got home from the festival, he found them there. Perhaps it did not make much difference, as I suppose none of us could have gone. But we should have been glad to make our own decision.

CHAPTER VIII.

TEN TIMES TEN MILLION.

SO the end comes of course. For when ten million people have determined that the right thing shall come to pass in this world, — having a good God on their side, they will always be found to have their own way. For reasons I have explained, the history becomes more vague. For we have now come to the period between 1879 and 1882, and the files of newspapers for that period, let us be thankful, are comparatively few. It was in the fall of 1879 that they gathered together under the fern leaves on Christmas Island.

But this *ten million* despatch gave spirit to all parties. And, over all the world, many a man and woman who had been talking prose all their lives, and doing very commonplace things, began to learn the great lessons, — that it is in the long-run much better to talk prose than to talk poetry, and that he who does commonplace things well may be mastering the world. With the ten million despatch, I should say, there came for the first time the feeling that even by prose and by commonplace the world might be saved.

And, for three years more, the three years between 1879 and 1882, the ten million people, each in his own home, were doing just what Harry himself did in the beginning. Only they had the feeling, now, that something was coming to pass which he never dreamed of, nor the Club of Ten, nor the Detroit Club. They did not put the " movement" into the newspaper; there was no " movement" to put in, — more than there was when Harry gave the Widow Corcoran her chips in the wood-shed. Still the great fact of the existence of the ten million could not well be kept out of the newspapers. And without dwelling on this period, I may just say that it was in these three years that the " movement," if it must be called so, went through the necessary crises of controversy.

Mr. Agassiz says that every great scientific truth goes through three stages. First, people say it conflicts with the Bible. Next, they say it had been discovered before. Lastly, they say they always believed it. Exactly this happened with the "movement." The first two stages came in, in the three years between 1879 and 1882.

As soon as the magic words,

TEN TIMES A MILLION IS TEN MILLION,'

appeared by direction of the local secretaries in the "Personal" of the daily newspapers, all the religious newspapers began inquiring into their meaning, — and to ask whether there were not concealed some profligate attack on the Bible. The particularly bright religious journals got leaders out about it within a fortnight after the words appeared, — the others not so soon. This delay was not amiss, however. The bright ones had all proved that the words were very dangerous, and that a terrible plot against the church was concealed in them. This waked up the drowsy ones, and they did not like to own that they had been asleep. So they all said they did not think the words were dangerous; the only danger was in the columns of the wakeful journals. This gave our friends one half the religious press as counsel for the defence; and as, in truth, our whole effort was in the simple line of the most unpretending Christianity, whenever any journal did try to rip up the constitution of a club, or to prove that Harry Wadsworth was a heathen, the effort generally came to grief of its own weight. There was a good deal of judicious comment on the dangers of secret societies, till it proved that none of the *ten million* people, as they came to be called, had formed any secret society. A good deal was said about log-rolling and mutual admiration societies. But on the whole it proved that they had a distaste for politics, and that when they were in public life they were men the public could not do without. Before many months, as it happened, a proposal was made in the English Parliament to omit the letter *u* from the spelling of "honour" in the English Bibles. And then on this question such a controversy arose in England as swept through the religious press of all the world, and this quite ended the "ten million discussion." Nothing more was ever said, so far as I ever heard, about the movement being hostile to the Bible.

But, on the other hand, a good many bright fellows, frontier bishops, secretaries of missionary societies, and such like, who were really trying, in their own way, to get the world forward if only they could find places for their levers, studied the bit of mathematics by which in twenty-one years seven zeroes had been annexed to the **1.** which stood for Harry Wadsworth. They had the wit to see that this was much more substantial victory than all their tracts had yet won,— or any one of their embassies. They saw at the same moment that it was precisely the system on which all Christian victories have been won,— on which the hundred people of the *Mayflower* cabin had become so many millions to-day. Hundreds of these men were sharp-sighted enough and faithful enough to claim the ten million as their own allies; and at once there were published millons of tracts with such titles as—

" HENRY WADSWORTH proved a SANDEMANIAN." Published by the Sandemanian Board. Price, one cent; one hundred and twenty-five copies for one dollar.

" TEN MILLION WITNESSES to the Articles of the Protestant Episcopal Church." Published for gratuitous distribution, with the authority of the Rt. Rev. Henry Cairns. Minneapolis, 1880.

"REASONS which make it evident that HENRY WADSWORTH was a Unitarian Congregational Christian." Tract No. 97. Sixth Series. American Unitarian Association, Chicago, 1881.

"WADSWORTH A UNIVERSALIST. A Short Tract, by Hiram Ballou. For circulation." Publishing House, New York, 1880.

"The Standards Planted. An Affectionate Appeal to the Ten Million." Philadelphia. Presbyterian Union, 1880.

"Wesley's Class System vindicated in Wadsworth's Tens." Methodist Board. New York, 1880.

And even Rome did not neglect an occasion so tempting; but there appeared "Religious Liberty the Method of the Holy Church: an Address to those who believe in the Four Detroit Mottoes." Catholic Publication House, New York, 1880.

All of them were eager to make out that the four Detroit Epigrams belonged specially to their own communions, and that the ten million would advance their central purpose by coming meekly into their respective organizations.

It was true enough that dear Harry had profited by all these people's books and plans. But Porter was all wrong, I am sorry to say, in pretending that Harry was a Sandemanian. The truth was, he was an officer of the Church of the Unity in Colchester; and, as such, he was at liberty to get all he could from Pope or from Pagan. In that Church, they never asked what a man believed, but they expected him to believe it with all his might, and no mistake. If he believed in Christ enough to come to their communion table, they never sought an excuse to turn him away.

So these three years sped by, — first, in the endeavor to show that the ten million were the most irreligious of men and women, which they were not; second, in an attempt from all the foci of ecclesiastical order to show that they were the most religious of men. To my notion they were, — though perhaps not exactly as these several tract-writers supposed.

Any way, religion or irreligion, the discussion did not help much, and did not hinder much, though perhaps it did hinder a little. The ten million were terribly in earnest, — just as much as the Original Ten were. Indeed, they were rather too much in earnest for any large scale frolic when the three years were over. I might say, rather, that in that summer, the summer of 1882, the whole civilized world seemed very much changed. Was it that so many men and women were caring for others more than themselves, and living for God's law and not for the Devil's? Any way, there was not a railroad accident in America or Europe that summer; Congress adjourned after a session of only three weeks, and most of the State legislatures after a session of only three days. In the pretty country jails they were taking summer boarders. None of the schools in America had any evening lessons. The daily newspapers all had feuilletons with continued stories in them, because they had neither murders, accidents, nor sensation trials. Coal was at half price, because they mined by machinery, and the workmen had forgotten the mystery of striking. There was not a village but had its daily afternoon jollification, with a play, or dance, or poem à la Morris, or charade, or picnic, or concert. And all life seemed such a frolic, that nobody cared to go to Baden-Baden or to Christmas Island, for a Conferenz or a Convention.

None the less did the local secretaries foot up their books, and telegraph the result to Dalrymple in Norfolk. Dalrymple's hair was iron-gray now, but he stepped with a firm gait, and his voice rang out as cheerily as ever. With such telegraphs as 1882 worked, his communication even with Timbuctoo was easy. Every day he received some dozens of despatches from different capitals; and at last, late in October, he got a despatch from Irkutsk informing him that an express was in from an outlying region of the Chalcha land among the Mongols. For this express they had been waiting, before they could send in their totals. And Dalrymple reverently added the figures to the sum of all the other stations which he had cast before. That total was 99,998,180

The Irkutsk despatch gave 24,792

So the grand total was 100,022,972 souls.

Horace, dear old boy, touched a key of his table telegraph, and in five seconds the bells of Swaffham, and Cockley, and Aylsham, and Dereham, and Hingham, and Norwich, and for aught I know, of half England, were chiming with triple bob-majors and every thing else that would express joy. Ten hours of joyful chiming in Norwich, before they brought the bells home! Horace touched another key, and sent his private despatch to young Gladstone, who was then in his father's place as First Lord of the Treasury. In five seconds more the Tower guns were firing, — nay, in ten seconds an imperial salute was firing from every battery in that empire on which the sun never sets. Napoleon IV. did not get his despatch for five minutes. He was riding in the Bois de Boulogne, and the "repeat" did not find him. But the Home Minister got his, and took the responsibility of ordering the French salutes. So that when Napoleon did get the paper, he knew what it was before he opened it.

It was all an affair of seconds over the world, announced at sunset, sunrise, noon, or midnight, according to your longitude. Our President then was a man you do not know, John Fisher. He was an enthusiast. And his arrangements for salutes were so perfect that he said there was not a capital city in America but knew the news sooner than Napoleon IV. had it. You see they had nothing to do, in those days, with the government stores of nitre and powder, but to burn it in jollification. So they burned it.

And thus it was an old story to most of the world when, the next morning, at the head of the "Personal" in the newspaper, men read —

TEN TIMES TEN MILLION IS A HUNDRED MILLION.

Dalrymple wrote me a philosophical letter this time. He confessed that he had been terribly frightened before the Irkutsk despatch came. As it was, he said, it was by the skin of our teeth we were saved. He bade me remark the falling off between 109,341,270, which, as he said, should have been the number, at the least, and 100,022,972, which it was. "It is all very well for the multitude," said he, "to say 'ten times ten million is a hundred million,' and that is, thank God, one of the eternal truths. But, for all that, we have not gained tenfold in these three years. We have fallen off badly. So much for the quarrels of you Dominies. All the time we were sticking fast on the Great Roll, at those ninety-seven millions and ninety-eight millions that filled up so slowly, my heart was in my throat. I lost my appetite, and could not hit a partridge if I tried. I tell you a million people are a great many. And when that plucky Tchitchakoft's bulletin came in, Fred, I could have kissed him. But, for the love of dear Harry, let us have no more quarrelling among you padres!"

CHAPTER IX.

A THOUSAND MILLION.

AND why were all these salutes fired, the world over? Why was every capital illuminated? Why was there a holiday given to every school? Half-holidays had been the universal daily custom for years before. It was simply, you see, that a tenth part of the people in the world had shown, in some way worth belief, that they meant —

To look up and not down,
To look forward and not back,
To look out and not in, —
 and
To lend a hand.

I say one tenth, in round numbers. We did not know in 1882 how many people there were in the world exactly. But we had subdued some estimates, and we had swelled some, and we "conceited" that there were rather more than a thousand million men, women, and children, the world over. We had one estimate as high as 1,228,000,000; and this was, for want of a better, taken by the statistical men as the true one. It was roughly said that a tenth part of these were those little children of whose like is the kingdom of heaven, who are not yet profaned by contact with earth, or who, at all events, cannot be pledged to any line of duty. If this were so, there were, in round hundreds, one thousand one hundred million sentient, sensible, and responsible people in the world, say over three years old. Now, one tenth of these, as I said, were willing to live for the company rather than themselves. This willingness started this rejoicing. Of course a minority so large as that, practically agreeing on a few principles, ruled absolutely the larger majority. When but one man in thirteen was a Christian in the Roman Empire, Constantine found it politic to proclaim Christianity.

But we meant no such flash in the pan as Constantine's proclamation. We had not seen the Club of ten enlarge to the hundred million, in less than a generation, to stop there. Indeed, the ten meanest men among those Chalcha people were as much in earnest as any of us of the Original Ten, that this world, and nothing less, should be put on a few simple principles, such as Jesus Christ lived for and died for. No man said any thing about this. The quarrels of the Dominies had cured us of talk and of new methods. Every man and woman understood that there was no short cut nor patent process. We saw that the thing must spread by contagion if it spread at all. Still, though no man said any thing, I can tell you the interest became intense, almost terrible sometimes, as those next three years whirled by.

You see at first these hundred million people were very unequally divided. Commerce, adventure, and all that, had scattered them a great deal; but still there were favored points and points not favored. There were whole villages, where, as far as you could see, almost every man held loyal to the Four Mottoes; where you were fairly tempted to say that God's own kingdom of love had come, just as you are tempted to say that of some Homes you and I know of.

But these people, if they really meant " to lend

a hand," could not stay in any such four-square Sybaris as that. Indeed they would stifle there, for want of vital air, and of exercise. They could not say their prayers there, indeed. What use in praying " Thy kingdom come, Thy will be done on earth as it is done in heaven," if they, the very work-people to whom God had intrusted the work of the world, were doing nothing about it? And of course, as they looked out and not in, and forward and not backward, they did not satisfy themselves with making a contribution in church to help send one man in a black frock coat and a white neck-cloth to do this thing for them. They went themselves, in great companies. That was the new school of missions which built up the new civilization: unless you remember Lord Baltimore, and Winthrop, and the *Mayflower*, or perhaps go back to Isocrates and Herodotus, and say it was the old school of missions. A new Sybaris, say better a new Nazareth, would plant itself right in the midst of a horde of Gauchos, with rifles enough to make itself respected, — yes, but with dolls and rattles enough for the Gaucho babies, bread and butter enough for the Gaucho women if there were famine, and, in general, love enough to tame any Gaucho chief who was not very thick-skinned. All over the world you saw such clusters of young people going from worn-out soils to the virgin soils, or from the new lands to the historical: Old and New playing into each other's hands, and, by wonderful combinations, taking tricks which had been thought impossible before.

Then you began to see the old line of public appeal exactly changed. The advertisement became the appeal of generosity instead of the plea of selfishness.

From the New York Herald.

A MOTHER and her daughter, without encumbrance, would gladly know where they can be of use. One of them was in Mrs. Emerson's school, and they have had the advantage of personal acquaintance with two of the Original Ten. Address M. and D., Herald Office.

FIVE young men, who graduate this summer at Cornell, would like to go to any part of the world where they are needed. Will bear their own expenses. Have heard the lectures of Mr. Widdifield, and the brothers Corcoran.

A WIDOW with four children will take into her family a paralyzed woman, or any blind person. Two sons good at lifting invalids. No charge for board, lodging, or washing. Address LAUNDRESS.

From the New York Observer.

DISTANCE no objection. Seven families, all the members of which are in good health and have lived together without quarrelling for seventeen years, will gladly go together to any outpost. None of them ever believed in total depravity. Address the Editor of this Journal.

SEVEN languages! Four gentlemen with their wives, in whose number are good interpreters in seven languages, are ready to sail at a moment's warning. No charge or salary. Have met personally five of the Original Ten. Address F. O. U. R.

DETROIT Club. Eleven members of the Original Detroit Club, with their families, wish to correspond with reference to duty. From an experience of twenty-four years, they are sure that they shall arouse no animosity among any Christians. Inquire of the Editor of the Observer.

THE graduates of Humboldt College, Iowa, of the present Senior Class — three hundred and seven in number — offer themselves for duty. Can work their way as stokers if necessary. They belong to one hundred and seven religious sects, and are yet to know their first dissension. If necessary, two hundred and ninety-four ladies can accompany them. Address Senior, Springvale, Humboldt, Iowa.

And so on, and so on. These are only a few out of hundreds. And they are enough to show you how the world is really turned round, when the people in it, instead of inquiring first about what they shall eat and drink, are inquiring first how the kingdom of God shall come.

And, I promise you, with such practical use of the machinery of daily life, the kingdom could be seen coming. The enlargement of the world, or of man's intercourse in the world, of course all the time made the world smaller. The telegraphs, the journeys back and forth to old homes, the enlargement of means of life and love, as the old war establishments were put down and the old taxes forgotten,— all these things brought Irkutsk and North Colchester very near each other; and it no longer seemed strange to find Harry's portrait in a sledge, as you drove across the Baikal.

Indeed, I believe that any true history of those years would show that the greatest difficulties were not among these distant people. For the first time in history, we began to get interesting letters from the outposts. You see, these people not looking in, but looking out, did not have to tell us much of their own headaches or heart-aches or belly-aches, but were able to devote all their pen, ink, and paper, to the things that they saw, which we at home wanted them to describe. They dealt largely with simple people, and it sometimes seemed as if their accounts were of a "nation in a day," as the hymn says; though really they caught all their converts with the hook, and not in a net. It was not on the out-skirts that the last difficulties were found. But as every man finds that the hardest knots he has to chop through are those which have been wait-ing in his own wood-shed while easier work was done, so it proved now, that the very hardest jobs of all were in some of the home stations, in breaking up hard-pan which we had been for generations trampling down.

Just one story of such difficulty, and the whole history of victory may be brought to an end.

It was in the spring of the last of those three years. Every thing seemed happy, smooth, contented, vigorous, and wise. Those of us who were in the movement — and who indeed was not? — could not find man, woman, or talking child, this land through, who was not somehow or other showing practical sympathy with us. I think it was rather as a jollification, than to point out any new line of work, that the "Reformed Association of Covenanters of the New Lanark Platform" held their great decennial convention at Sherman City. This, you know, was one of the most important ecclesiastical gatherings that we could have in this country. The newspapers had so little else to tell that they all had reporters there. Seven hundred clergy and fourteen hundred lay delegates were in attendance. The meeting was held in a Rink, with temporary seats, so that every thing seemed to promise a happy time. Never did a more plucky or manly set of fellows bear cross on their shoulders than the men I knew who were in that convention. By way of doing honor to age and experience and learning, old Dr. Philpotts had been appointed president, and he was to preach the opening sermon.

Imagine, then, the haggard dismay of all

parties, — press, town, delegates, everybody, — when the old gentleman gave out his text, "And what concord hath Christ with Belial?" (2 Cor. v. 15), and proceeded, in the most systematic way, to "pitch in" to the four Detroit mottoes! First, he should show that it was impossible for a regenerate man to look up, and that his duty was to look down. "Why stand ye gazing up into heaven?" (Acts i. 11.) Second, he should show that every regenerate man must look backward rather than forward. "Remember the days of darkness." (Eccl. xi. 8.) Third, he should show that every regenerate man must commune first with his own soul. "While I was musing, the fire burned." (Ps. xxxix. 3.) Fourth, and lastly, that all the dangers at which he had hinted were slight indeed compared with that Covenant of Works, in which men were tempted to suppose that they could advance or hinder the Creator's plans. "A fox shall break down their stone wall." (Nehemiah iv. 3.) If you live to 1885, you will perhaps fall in with this celebrated sermon in print. I spare you the detail, therefore. About the close there was no "if."

"You have observed, my friends, that I have

considered the fittest subject of our meditations on this occasion to be a series of fascinating errors, which have led astray a few giddy young men, in the thought or hope that they had found out a better gospel! Let us all hope that these straws of human harvesting may be blown away even as chaff by the wind of the Infinite Spirit. For myself, as the representative of this august assembly,—though these were to be my last words,—looking round upon the sacrilegious mottoes which deform and deface the Hall in which we are assembled, I declare that I will never accept them as principles of conduct— never, never, never!" And with this outburst he sat down.

In fact, when Vittermayer had painted the Rink in real fresco, he had wrought in the four mottoes on the four walls. By this time they were so universal that you saw them everywhere.

People were aghast! There was not a human being in the assembly, except the good old Doctor, who was not up to his eyes in the determination that this world should be made a world of Faith, Hope, and Love. So indeed was he.

But he had found it necessary to make his individual and loyal protest against the way things were going on, because they were rather different from the way he supposed they went on in the Covenanters' time. There was a horrid hush for a moment, and then Wilderspin stepped forward and gave out, —

"Had I the tongues of Greeks and Jews,"

to be sung by the congregation. They sung it with a will, and blew off steam a little so. Wilderspin invoked a benediction, and they went sadly home.

Then began synods, and committees, and every sort of mutual conference, to make the old Doctor back down. "Think how it will sound among those nice Bamangwato people," said my Pauline; and everybody had some like feeling. But the old man was flint. They got him, at last, to say in a letter, that, in a modified sense, a Christian might look up to God without stepping off the platform of the Reformed Covenanters, which was the great object with him, — then that he might forget himself, without dangerous sin, — and that he even ought to look forward to a happier future; but, as to "lending a hand," never! cried the old man. "It is a Covenant of Works, and union with the Devil."

So sadly came the October in which we had hoped so much. All the other secretaries reported a world subdued by Love. In all the other continents men had found some way to express this Love, and the Faith and Hope which were intertwined with it. All princes and all people were hoping and praying that, as October passed away, one joyful signal the world over might show that the horrors of old history were sealed in one tomb, and that in one unanimous heart-beat a world of self-forgetting men would begin to live as one hearty family of God! But here was one man, who with the noblest motive cried out, " Never, never, never!" Whatever else might happen, he would never say he would " lend a hand."

The thirty-first day of October dawned. I will confess that it was a sad day. Newman wrote me that to him it was a bitter morning. He had been all the evening before discussing the Monophysite heresy with Dr. Philpotts. "I had forgotten the hated names for years," wrote poor Newman; and so he had led round to the beauty of Unity among Brethren, to which the old man had assented sweetly; and then Newman had asked, timidly, if, with a change of the language, he could not bring his heart to agree to "do good as he had opportunity"? "Covenant of Works!" said the old Trojan; "Never, never, never!" So Newman went home, and so waked sadly. A sad breakfast. None of them could get to work. And Newman wrote me that he thanked God even when he heard the fire-alarm strike, because it was an excuse for him to leave his study.

But when he came to the district, he bitterly rued that selfish thought. The fire was a sudden and bad one. It was already checked below, but smoke was pouring up and out of the attic windows of the warehouse or factory where it had been burning. It proved to be a factory of paper-boxes, and the pasting women in the attics had been stifling from the smoke. They lay out on the steep roof, with their feet stayed in the gutters, when Newman came there. George Davis and Lawrence Flaherty were moving heaven and earth to bring their ladders to the eaves, — and did so; but no man could stand the smoke, as he ran up, — far less did those poor girls dare to risk it, coming down. Newman told me he saw five fellows in succession dash up Flaherty's ladder, waver, and lose their heads, and drop senseless into the arms of the crowd below. At last flames began to break out of the fourth-story window, and to lap and lick up the outside of the building. Three minutes, and the whole would be over, — when a tall-man, in his shirt-sleeves, ran boldly down the slope of the roof of the church next the factory; by an easy spring jumped across the five-feet chasm between the buildings, walked like a cat to the dormer behind which these five girls were crouching; and then could be seen leading them, lifting them, encouraging; and then actually carrying one along the giddy gutter-edge, till he had led them all to the more sheltered side upon which he had sprung. Davis had caught the idea already; and, by the time that last faint child was on that side, Davis himself was at his ladder's top to take her. One, two, three, — all five passed down, — and then Shirt-sleeves, as the crowd called him, sprang back across the gulf to the church-roof; and running up the slates to the tower, slipped in, and disappeared. The whole throng was cheering and yelling. The girls were taken, I know not how, — and tended, I know not by whom. Everybody but Davis and Flaherty seemed to forget the fire; and Newman found himself (as I suppose every one did) asking who Shirt-sleeves was, and where he had gone. The general impression was, seeing he had come down from the steeple, that he was an angel in shirt-sleeves. Talk grew loud at the church-door, which proved to be locked. At last the fussy, lazy sexton appeared on the steps, trying, by his air, to make people think that he was virtually the hero of the occasion, though he had not happened to do that particular deed. "Hannay," cried Newman, "is that you? who was the man, — where is he?"

"Locked up in his study," said Hannay; "sees no one till office-hour."

"Study?" cried Newman. "Who do you say it is?"

"Why, don't *you* know?" says Hannay. "Guess you don't see him in his shirt-sleeves as often as I do. He saws all the wood for the furnace fires. Why, it is the old Doctor!"

Newman turned to the crowd, waved his hand, and cried, " Three times three for Dr. Philpotts! " And did they not cheer well?

Yes: the stanch old theologian, who would have died before he would accept a " Covenant of Works," had risked his life, without one anxious thought, for those five girls. " A trick I learned when I was unregenerate," he said afterwards. " I was an undergraduate at Cambridge, and had some duties to discharge in taking the tongue out from the chapel bell."

And the Sherman City papers stopped the press, and put in EXTRAS, to announce " Gallantry of Dr. Philpotts! " " Dr. Philpotts *lends a hand!* " And the local secretary telegraphed to the Middle States Secretary, and he telegraphed to the Central Union Secretary, and he telegraphed to Dalrymple, —

" Dr. Philpotts has lent a hand! "

And this was all anybody was waiting for. And before noon of that day, the Brothers in Unity at Fort Grant were firing a salute from the two cannon left for that purpose; so that when the Doctor's study was open at his office-hour, he and all men knew that the whole world was One. The old gentleman was overwhelmed with visitors. He received their congratulations and thanks cordially; but he said, "I have not acceded, and I never will accede, to a Covenant of Works."

That day the whole world held festival. All schools were dismissed, all banks and workshops and factories closed, — all " unnecessary labor suspended," — as the great salutes and the great chimes came booming out, which announced the agreement of a world of self-forgetting men. That day do I say? Every day from that day was festival, century after century. So soon as the world once learned the infinite blessing of Active Love, and stayed it by Faith, and enjoyed it in Hope, there was no danger that the world should unlearn that lesson.

That lesson — if this vision of a possibility prove true — comes to the world by no change of law, by no new revelation, nor other gospel than the world has now. It comes simply as man after man, and woman after woman, lead such unselfish lives as all of us see sometimes, as all would be glad to live, as dear Harry Wadsworth led while his short life went on.

Nine triads of years were enough each to add a zero to the figure which stood for that one man.

Ten times one was ten, $10 \times 1 = 10$. There was one zero.

But as the nine zeroes were added, in twenty-seven years the **1.** became 1,000,000,000 — **ONE THOUSAND MILLION.**

This proved to be the number of the Happy World!

NEW BOOKS

FOR THE

AUTUMN AND WINTER OF 1870–71.

JEAN INGELOW. THE MONITIONS OF THE UNSEEN, AND OTHER NEW POEMS, including a Christmas Poem called "The Mariner's Cave." The book will be beautifully illustrated, and will be ready Dec. 1.

SYLVESTER JUDD. MARGARET. A Tale of the Real and the Ideal, of Blight and Bloom. 16mo. Price $1.50.

EDWARD E. HALE. TEN TIMES ONE IS TEN. The Possible Reformation. A Story. 16mo. Price $1.25.

HARRIET W. PRESTON. ASPENDALE: A STORY AND AN ESSAY. 16mo. Price $1.50.

ARTHUR HELPS. ESSAYS WRITTEN IN THE INTERVALS OF BUSINESS. To which is added "Organization in Daily Life." 16mo. Price $1.50.

ARTHUR HELPS. SHORT ESSAYS AND APHORISMS. 16mo.

WALTER SAVAGE LANDOR. PERICLES AND ASPASIA 16mo. Price $1.50.

J. R. SEELEY. (Author of "Ecce Homo.") ROMAN IMPERIALISM, and other Papers. 16mo. Price $1.50

J. R. SEELEY. LECTURES ON ROMAN HISTORY. 16mo.

PAUL KONEWKA. SILHOUETTE ILLUSTRATIONS TO GOETHE'S FAUST, with English text from Bayard Taylor's new Translation. One elegant quarto. Price $4.00.

JOHN WHOPPER'S ADVENTURES. With Illustrations.

Published by ROBERTS BROTHERS,
BOSTON

143, WASHINGTON STREET, BOSTON
Autumn and Winter of 1870–71.

MESSRS. ROBERTS BROTHERS'
GENERAL LIST OF WORKS.

☞ *The Books in this List, unless otherwise specified, are bound in Cloth. All of our Publications mailed, post-paid, on receipt of price.*

ALCOTT (LOUISA M.). Little Women; or, Meg, Jo, Beth and Amy. With Illustrations. Two volumes, 16mo. $3.00.

——— Hospital Sketches and Camp and Fireside Stories. With Illustrations. 16mo. $1.50.

——— An Old-Fashioned Girl. With Illustrations. 16mo. $1.50.

ALCOTT (A. BRONSON). Tablets. 16mo. $1.50.

ALGER (W. R.). The Poetry of the Orient. 16mo. $1.75.

——— A Critical History of the Doctrine of a Future Life. 8vo. $3.50.

——— The Solitudes of Nature and of Man; or, The Loneliness of Human Life. 16mo. $2.00.

——— The Friendships of Women. 16mo. $2.00.

——— Prayers offered in the Massachusetts House of Representatives during the Session of 1868. 16mo. $1.50.

ANGELS (THE) OF HEAVEN. Meditations on the Records of Angelic Visitation and Ministry contained in Scripture. With 12 Photographs. Small 4to. $6.00.

AUERBACH (BERTHOLD). On the Heights. 16mo. $2.00.

——— Villa Eden: The Country-House on the Rhine. 8vo. $2.00.

——— Edelweiss. 16mo. $1.00.

——— German Tales. 16mo. $1.00.

BALLANTYNE (R. M.). Gascoyne, the Sandal-Wood Trader. Illustrated. 16mo. $1.50.

LIST OF WORKS 3

BARING-GOULD (S.). Curious Myths of the Middle Ages.
16mo. $1.50.

BARNES (WM.). Rural Poems. With 12 full-page Illustrations. Square 16mo. Bevelled cloth, gilt edges. $2.50.
Handy Volume Edition, $1.25.

BLACKFORD (MRS.). The Scottish Orphans; and Arthur Monteith. Illustrated. 16mo. 75 cents.

BROOKS (CHARLES T.). The Layman's Breviary; or, Meditations for Every Day in the Year. From the German of Leopold Schefer. 16mo. $2.50. A cheaper edition, $1.50

BUCHANAN'S (ROBERT) POEMS. 16mo. $1.75.

BURNAND (F. C.). Happy Thoughts. 16mo. $1.00.

BUTLER (SAMUEL). Hudibras. With Notes, a Life of the Author, and Illustrations. 32mo. $1.25.

BUONAPARTE (NAPOLEON). Table Talk and Opinions of. 18mo. $1.25.

CERVANTES (MIGUEL DE). The Adventures of Don Quixote De La Mancha. Translated by Charles Jarvis. Illustrated. Small Quarto. $8.00.

COWLEY (ABRAHAM). Essays. With Life by the Editor, Notes and Illustrations by Dr. HURD, and others. 18mo. $1.25.

DALTON (WM.). The Tiger Prince; or, Adventures in the Wilds of Abyssinia. Illustrated. 16mo. $1.50.

DAY (THOMAS). Sandford and Merton. Illus'd. 16mo. $1.25.

DAVY (SIR H.) Consolations in Travel; or, The Last Days of a Philosopher. 16mo. $1.50.

—— Salmonia; or, Days of Fly-Fishing. 16mo. $1.50.

EDWARDS (M. BETHAM). Doctor Jacob. A Novel. $1.00.

FITZGERALD (PERCY). Autobiography of a Small Boy. Illustrated. 16mo. $2.00.

FROLICH (L.). Picture-Book, Mischievous John, Foolish Zôe, Boasting Hector. The Text by their Mammas; the Designs by L. FROLICH. Small quarto. $2.00.

GOETHE'S Hermann and Dorothea. Translated by ELLEN FROTHINGHAM. Illustrated. Thin 8vo. $2.00. Cheap Ed. $1.00.

GRAY'S (DAVID) POEMS. With an Introductory Notice by Lord Houghton, Memoir of the Author, and Final Memorials. 16mo. $1.50.

GREENWELL (DORA). Carmina Crucis. 16mo. $1.50.

GRISET'S (ERNEST) GROTESQUES; or, Jokes Drawn on Wood. With Rhymes by TOM HOOD. One hundred quaint designs. Small quarto. $3.75.

HAMERTON (PHILIP G.). A Painter's Camp. Book I.: In England. Book II.: In Scotland. Book III.: In France. 16mo. $1.50.

HEDGE (F. H.). The Primeval World of Hebrew Tradition. 16mo. $1.50.

HELPS (ARTHUR). Realmah. 16mo. $2.00.

—— Casimir Maremma. 16mo. $2.00.

—— Companions of My Solitude. 16mo. $1.50.

HELEN AND HER COUSINS; or, Two Months at Ashfield Rectory. 18mo. 50 cents.

HEAVEN (THE) SERIES. 16mo. Each, $1.25.
HEAVEN OUR HOME. We have no Saviour but Jesus, and no Home but Heaven.
MEET FOR HEAVEN. A State of Grace upon Earth the only Preparation for a State of Glory in Heaven.
LIFE IN HEAVEN. There Faith is changed into Sight, and Hope is passed into Blissful Fruition.

HOPE (A. R.). A Book about Dominies. 16mo. $1.25.

—— A Book about Boys. 16mo. $1.25.

HOWITT (MARY). Fireside Tales. In Prose and Verse. 16mo. 75 cents.

HUNT (LEIGH). The Book of the Sonnet. 2 vols. $3.00.

—— The Seer; or, Common Places Refreshed. 2 vols 16mo. $3.00.

—— A Day by the Fire, and other Papers hitherto uncollected. Edited by "TOM FOLIO." 16mo. $1.50.

INGELOW'S (JEAN) POEMS. 2 vols. 16mo. $3.50.
2 vols. 32mo. $3.00.
1 vol. 16mo. Cabinet Edition. $2.25.
Illustrated Edition. 8vo. $12.00.
SONGS OF SEVEN. Illustrated. 8vo. $5.00.

—— PROSE. Studies for Stories. Illustrated. 16mo. $1.50.
STORIES TOLD TO A CHILD. Illustrated. 16mo. $1.25.
A SISTER'S BYE-HOURS. Illustrated. 16mo. $1.25.
MOPSA THE FAIRY. A Story. Illustrated. 16mo. $1.25.
POOR MATT; or, The Clouded Intellect. 18mo. 60 cents.

INGRAHAM'S (J. H.) WORKS. 3 vols. 12mo. Each, $2.
THE PRINCE OF THE HOUSE OF DAVID; or, Three Years in the Holy City.
THE PILLAR OF FIRE; or, Israel in Bondage.
THE THRONE OF DAVID,—from the Consecration of the Shepherd of Bethlehem to the Rebellion of Prince Absalom.

"JANUS." The Pope and the Council. Authorized Translation from the German. 16mo. $1.50.

JOINVILLE (THE SIRE DE). Saint Louis, King of France. Translated by JAMES HUTTON. 18mo. $1.25.

LAMB (CHARLES). A Memoir. By BARRY CORNWALL. 16mo. $1.75.

LETTERS EVERYWHERE. Stories and Rhymes for Children. 28 Illustrations. Square 8vo. $3.00.

LIBRARY OF EXEMPLARY WOMEN. 6 vols. 12mo. Each, $2.00.
MEMOIRS AND CORRESPONDENCE OF MADAME RECAMIER. Translated and Edited by Miss LUYSTER.
THE FRIENDSHIPS OF WOMEN. By Rev. W. R. ALGER.
LIFE AND LETTERS OF MADAME SWETCHINE. By COUNT DE FALLOUX. Translated by Miss PRESTON.
SAINTE-BEUVE'S PORTRAITS OF CELEBRATED WOMEN. Translated by Miss PRESTON.
THE LETTERS OF MADAME DE SÉVIGNÉ. Edited, with a Memoir, by Mrs. SARAH J. HALE.
THE LETTERS OF LADY MARY WORTLEY MONTAGU. Edited, with a Memoir, by Mrs. SARAH J. HALE.

LUYSTER (I. M.). Miss Lily's Voyage Round the World. Undertaken in company with her two cousins, Masters Paul and Toto, and Little Peter. Translated from the French by Miss Luyster. 48 designs by Lorenz Frolich. 8vo. $3.50.

—— The Little Gypsy. Translated from the French of Eli Sauvage, by Miss Luyster. Illustrated. Square 12mo. $1.50.

6 PUBLISHED BY ROBERTS BROTHERS.

LYTTON'S (BULWER) DRAMAS AND POEMS. Containing "The Lady of Lyons," "Richelieu," and "Money," and Minor Poems. With a fine Portrait on Steel. One volume, 32mo. Blue and Gold. $1.25.

MACGREGOR (JOHN). A Thousand Miles in the Rob Roy Canoe; or, Rivers and Lakes of Europe. Map and Illustrations. 16mo. $2.50.

—— The Rob Roy on the Baltic: The Narrative of the Rob Roy Canoe, on Lakes and Rivers of Sweden, Denmark, Norway, and on the Baltic and North Seas. Illustrated. 16mo. $2.50.

—— The Voyage Alone in the Yawl "Rob Roy," from London to Paris, and back by Havre, the Isle of Wight, South Coast, etc. 16mo. $2.50.

MARRYATT (CAPT.). The Privateersman. Adventures by Sea and Land. Illustrated. 16mo. $1.50.

MAX (LITTLE). With fifteen Etchings, by RUDOLF GEISSLER. 4to. $2.50.

MORRIS (WILLIAM). The Earthly Paradise. Parts I. and II. Spring and Summer periods. Crown 8vo., $3.00. 16mo. $2.25.

—— The Earthly Paradise. Part III. Autumn period. Crown 8vo., $3.00. 16mo., $2.25.

—— The Earthly Paradise. Part IV. Winter period. (In preparation.)

—— The Life and Death of Jason. A Poem. 16mo. $1.50.

—— The Lovers of Gudrun. With Frontispiece from Designs by Billings. 16mo. Price $1.00.

MOUNTAIN ADVENTURES in the various Countries of the World. Selected from the Narratives of Celebrated Travellers. Illustrations. 12mo. $2.50.

NEAL (JOHN). Wandering Recollections of a Somewhat Busy Life. An Autobiography. 16mo. $2.00.

—— Great Mysteries and Little Plagues. A Story-book for Young and Old. 16mo. $1.25.

PALGRAVE (F. T.). The Five Days' Entertainments at Wentworth Grange. With Original Designs by ARTHUR HUGHES. 8vo. $4.00.

PARKER (JOSEPH). Ecce Deus: Essays on the Life and
Doctrine of Jesus Christ. With Controversial Notes on " Ecce Homo."
16mo. $1.50

PAUL PRESTON'S VOYAGES, Travels and Remarkable
Adventures. Illustrated. 16mo. $1.25.

PENNIMAN (MAJOR). The Tanner Boy. A Life of General Grant. Illustrated. 16mo. $1.50.

POPULAR FAIRY TALES. Containing the choicest and best
known Fairy Stories. Illustrated. 2 vols. 16mo. Each, $1.25.

PELLICO (SILVIO). My Prisons. Memoirs of SILVIO PELLICO. With an Introduction by Epes Sargent. 12mo $3.50. A
cheaper edition, $1.75.

PRENTISS (E.). Nidworth and his Three Magic Wands. 16mo.
$1.25.

PUTNAM (E. T. H.). Where is the City? The experience of
a young man in search of the true Church; with sketches of the
Baptists, Congregationalists, Methodists, Episcopalians, Quakers, Swedenborgians, Spiritualists, Universalists, and Unitarians. 16mo. $1.50.

PUNSHON (W. MORLEY). The Prodigal Son. Four Discourses, with a Preface by Rev. GILBERT HAVEN. 16mo. 50 cents.
(Paper covers, 25 cents.)

ROSSETTI'S (C. G.) POEMS. With Four Designs by D. G.
ROSSETTI. 16mo. $1.75.

ROSSETTI'S (DANTE GABRIEL) POEMS. 16mo. $1.50.

SAND (GEORGE). Mauprat. A Novel. Translated by VIRGINIA VAUGHAN. 16mo. $1.50

—— Antonia. A Novel. Translated by VIRGINIA VAUGHAN.
16mo. $1.50.

—— Monsieur Sylvestre. A Novel. Translated by FRANCIS
G. SHAW. 16mo. $1.50.

—— The Snow Man. Translated by VIRGINIA VAUGHAN.
16mo. $1.50.

—— The Miller of Angibault. Translated by M. E. DEWEY.
16mo. $1.50.

SARGENT (EPES). The Woman who Dared. A Poem. 16mo.
$1.50.

—— Planchette; or, The Despair of Science. Being a full
account of Modern Spiritualism. 16mo. $1.25.

SCHEFER (LEOPOLD). The Layman's Breviary. A Selection for Every Day in the Year. Translated from the German by CHARLES T. BROOKS. 16mo. $2.50. A cheaper edition, $1.50.

SCHILLER'S LAY OF THE BELL. Translated by BULWER. The Designs by MORITZ RETZSCH. Oblong 4to. $7.50.

(SEELEY, J. R.?). Ecce Homo. A Survey of the Life and Work of Jesus Christ. 16mo. $1.50.

SHAKESPEARE'S WORKS. The Globe Edition. With all the Poems and a Glossary. 16mo. $2.00.

SHAKESPEARE'S MIDSUMMER-NIGHT'S DREAM. With 24 Silhouette Illustrations by P. KONEWKA. Royal 8vo. $5.00.

SHENSTONE (WILLIAM). Essays on Men and Manners. 16mo. $1.25.

STEINMETZ (A.). Sunshine and Showers: Their Influences throughout Creation. A Compendium of Popular Meteorology. 8vo. With Illustrations. $3.00.

SWAIN'S (CHARLES) POEMS. 32mo. $1.25.

SWETCHINE'S (MADAME) WRITINGS. Edited by the COUNT DE FALLOUX. Translated by H. W. PRESTON. 16mo. $1.50.

TIMB'S (JOHN). Eccentricities of the Animal Creation. With Eight Engravings. 12mo. $2.50.

TRENCH (W. S.). Realities of Irish Life. 16mo. $1.00.

TYTLER (SARAH). Sweet Counsel. A Book for Girls. 16mo. $1.50.

WALFORD (E.). The Story of the Chevalier Bayard. 18mo. $1.25.

WOMEN (THE) OF THE OLD TESTAMENT. Meditations on some Traits of Feminine Characters recorded in Sacred History. With Twelve Photographs. Small 4to. $6.00.

YONGE (MISS). The Pigeon Pie. A Tale of Roundhead Times. 16mo. $1.25.

Messrs. ROBERTS BROTHERS' Publications are for sale by all Booksellers and News Dealers, and will be mailed, post-paid, on receipt of the price, by the Publishers.

GEORGE SAND'S NOVELS.

I. MAUPRAT. Translated by VIRGINIA VAUGHAN.
II. ANTONIA. Translated by VIRGINIA VAUGHAN.
III. MONSIEUR SYLVESTRE. Translated by FRANCIS GEORGE SHAW.
IV. L'HOMME DE NEIGE. (The Man of Snow.) Translated by VIRGINIA VAUGHAN.

(OTHERS IN PREPARATION.)

A standard Library Edition, uniformly bound, in neat 16mo volumes. Each volume sold separately. Price $1.50.

SOME NOTICES OF "MAUPRAT."

"An admirable translation. As to 'Mauprat,' with which novel Roberts Brothers introduce the first of French novelists to the American public, if there were any doubts as to George Sand's power, it would for ever set them at rest. . . . The object of the story is to show how, by her (Edmée's) noble nature, he (Mauprat) is subsequently transformed from a brute to a man; his sensual passion to a pure and holy love." — *Harper's Monthly.*

"The excellence of George Sand, as we understand it, lies in her comprehension of the primitive elements of mankind. She has conquered her way into the human heart, and whether it is at peace or at war, is the same to her; for she is mistress of all its moods. No woman before ever painted the passions and the emotions with such force and fidelity, and with such consummate art. Whatever else she may be, she is always an artist. . . . Love is the key-note of 'Mauprat,' — love, and what it can accomplish in taming an otherwise untamable spirit. The hero, Bernard Mauprat, grows up with his uncles, who are practically bandits, as was not uncommon with men of their class, in the provinces, before the breaking out of the French Revolution. He is a young savage, of whom the best that can be said is, that he is only less wicked than his relatives, because he has somewhere within him a sense of generosity and honor, to which they are entire strangers. To sting this sense into activity, to detect the makings of a man in this brute, to make this brute into a man, is the difficult problem, which is worked out by love, — the love of Bernard for his cousin Edmée, and hers for him, — the love of two strong, passionate, noble natures, locked in a life-and-death struggle, in which the man is finally overcome by the unconquerable strength of womanhood. Only a great writer could have described such a struggle, and only a great artist could have kept it within allowable limits. This George Sand has done, we think; for her portrait of Bernard is vigorous without being coarse, and her situations are strong without being dangerous. Such, at least, is the impression we have received from reading 'Mauprat,' which, besides being an admirable study of character, is also a fine picture of French provincial life and manners." — *Putnam's Monthly.*

"Roberts Brothers propose to publish a series of translations of George Sand's better novels. We can hardly say that all are worth appearing in English; but it is certain that the 'better' list will comprise a good many which are worth translating, and among these is 'Mauprat,' — though by no means the best of them. Written to show the possibility of constancy in man, a love inspired before and continuing through marriage, it is itself a contradiction to a good many of the popular notions respecting the author, — who is generally supposed to be as indifferent to the sanctities of the marriage relation as was her celebrated ancestor, Augustus of Saxony. . . . The translation is admirable. It is seldom that one reads such good English in a work translated from any language. The new series is inaugurated in the best possible way, under the hands of Miss Vaughan, and we trust that she may have a great deal to do with its continuance. It is not every one who can read French who can write English so well." — *Old and New.*

Sold everywhere by the Publishers, Mailed, postpaid, on receipt of the advertised price,

ROBERTS BROTHERS, BOSTON.

ARTHUR HELPS'S WRITINGS.

1. REALMAH. A Story. Price $2.00.
2. CASIMIR MAREMMA. A Novel. Price $2.00.
3. COMPANIONS OF MY SOLITUDE. Price $1.50.
4. ESSAYS WRITTEN IN THE INTERVALS OF BUSINESS. Price $1.50.

From the London Review.

"The tale (REALMAH) is a comparatively brief one, intersected by the conversations of a variety of able personages, with most of whose names and characters we are already familiar through 'Friends in Council.' Looking at it in connection with the social and political lessons that are wrapt up in it, we may fairly attribute to it a higher value than could possibly attach to a common piece of fiction."

From a Notice by Miss E. M. Converse.

"There are many reasons why we like this irregular book (Realmah), in which we should find the dialogue tedious without the story; the story dull without the dialogue; and the whole unmeaning, unless we discerned the purpose of the author underlying the lines, and interweaving, now here, now there, a criticism, a suggestion, an aphorism, a quaint illustration, an exhortation, a metaphysical deduction, or a moral inference.

"We like a book in which we are not bound to read consecutively, whose leaves we can turn at pleasure and find on every page something to amuse, interest, and instruct. It is like a charming walk in the woods in early summer, where we are attracted now to a lowly flower half hidden under soft moss; now to a shrub brilliant with showy blossoms; now to the grandeur of a spreading tree; now to a bit of fleecy cloud; and now to the blue of the overarching sky.

"We gladly place 'Realmah' on the 'book-lined wall,' by the side of other chosen friends, — the sharp, terse sayings of the 'Doctor'; the suggestive utterances of the 'Noctes'; the sparkling and brilliant thoughts of 'Montaigne'; and the gentle teachings of the charming 'Elia.'"

From a Notice by Miss H. W. Preston.

"It must be because the reading world is unregenerate that Arthur Helps is not a general favorite. Somebody once said (was it Ruskin, at whose imperious order so many of us read 'Friends in Council,' a dozen years ago?) that appreciation of Helps is a sure test of culture. Not so much that, one may suggest, as of a certain native fineness and excellence of mind. The impression prevails among some of those who do not read him, that Helps is a hard writer. Nothing could be more erroneous. His manner is simplicity itself; his speech always winning, and of a silvery distinctness. There are hosts of ravenous readers, lively and capable, who, if their vague prejudice were removed, would exceedingly enjoy the gentle wit, the unassuming wisdom, and the refreshing originality of the author in question. There are men and women, mostly young, with souls that sometimes weary of the serials, who need nothing so much as a persuasive guide to the study of worthier and more enduring literature. For most of those who read novels with avidity are capable of reading something else with avidity, if they only knew it. And such a guide, and pleasantest of all such guides, is Arthur Helps. * * Yet 'Casimir Maremma' is a charming book, and, better still, invigorating. Try it. You are going into the country for the summer months that remain. Have 'Casimir' with you, and have 'Realmah,' too. The former is the pleasanter book, the latter the more powerful. But if you like one you will like the other. At the least you will rise from their perusal with a grateful sense of having been received for a time into a select and happy circle, where intellectual breeding is perfect, and the struggle for brilliancy unknown.

Sold everywhere. Mailed, post-paid, on receipt of advertised price, by the Publishers,

ROBERTS BROTHERS, BOSTON.

MARGARET.

By Sylvester Judd.   One volume.   Price $1.50.

SELECTIONS FROM SOME NOTABLE REVIEWS.

From the Southern Quarterly Review.

"This book, more than any other that we have read, leads us to believe in the possibility of a distinctive American Literature. . . . It bears the impress of New England upon all its features. It will be called the Yankee novel, and rightly; for nowhere else have we seen the thought, dialect, and customs of a New England Village, so well and faithfully represented. . . . More significant to our mind than any book that has yet appeared in our country. To us it seems to be a prophecy of the future. It contemplates the tendencies of American life and character. Nowhere else have we seen, so well written out, the very feelings which our rivers and woods and mountains are calculated to awaken. . . . We predict the time when Margaret will be one of the Antiquary's text-books. It contains a whole magazine of curious relics and habits. . . . as a record of great ideas and pure sentiments, we place it among the few great books of the age."

From the North American Review.

"We know not where any could go to find more exact and pleasing descriptions of the scenery of New England, or of the vegetable and animal forms which give it life. . . . As a representation of manners as they were, and in many respects are still, in New England, this book is of great value."

From the London Athenæum.

"This book, though published some time since in America, has only recently become known here by a few stray copies that have found their way over. Its leading idea is so well worked out, that, with all its faults of detail, it strikes us as deserving a wider circulation. . . . The book bears the impress of a new country, and is full of rough, uncivilized, but vigorous life. The leading idea which it seems intended to expound is, that the surest way to degrade men is to make themselves degraded; that so long as that belief does not poison the sources of experience, 'all things'—even the sins, follies, mistakes, so rife among men—can be made 'to work together for good.' This doctrine, startling as it may sound at first, is wrought out with a fine knowledge of human nature."

From the Anti-Slavery Standard.

"A remarkable book, with much good common sense in it, full of deep thought, pervaded throughout with strong religious feeling, a full conception of the essence of Christianity, a tender compassion for the present condition of man, and an abiding hope through love of what his destiny may be. . . . But all who, like Margaret, 'dream dreams,' and 'see visions,' and look for that time to come when man shall have 'worked out his own salvation,' and peace shall reign on earth, and good-will to men, will, if they can pardon the faults of the book for its merit, read it with avidity and pleasure."

From the Boston Daily Advertiser.

"This is quite a remarkable book, reminding you of Southey's 'Doctor,' perhaps, more than of any other book. . . . Margaret is a most angelic being, who loves everybody and whom everybody loves, and whose sweet influence is felt wherever she appears. She has visions of ideal beauty, and her waking eyes see beauty and joy in every thing."

From the Christian Register.

"This is a remarkable book. Its scene is laid in New England, and its period some half century ago. Its materials are drawn from the most familiar elements of every-day life. Its merits are so peculiar, and there is so much that is original and rich in its contents, that, sooner or later, it will be appreciated. It is impossible to predict with assurance the fate of a book, but we shall be much mistaken if Margaret does not in due season work its way to a degree of admiration seldom attained by a work of its class."

Sold everywhere. Mailed, prepaid, on receipt of price, by the Publishers,

Messrs. Roberts Brothers' Publications.

ECCE HOMO. A Survey of the Life and Work of Jesus Christ. In one volume, 16mo. Price, $1.50.

"It will do a service among a very large class of readers, such as are assigned to hardly more than two or three volumes in a century." — *Rev. George E. Ellis.*

"This remarkable book is one of those which permanently influence public opinion. The author has a right to claim deference from those who think deepest and know most, when he pleads before them that not Philosophy can save and reclaim the world, but Faith in a Divine Person who is worthy of it, allegiance to a Divine Society which He founded, and union of hearts in the object for which He created it." — *The Guardian.*

ECCE DEUS: Essays on the Life and Doctrine of Jesus Christ. With Controversial Notes on Ecce Homo. In one volume, to match Ecce Homo. Price, $1.50.

"We believe that many of the most grateful and consenting readers of 'Ecce Homo' will also be the most admiring readers of 'Ecce Deus.' In the main tenor of both the volumes there is nothing to our minds inconsistent. . . . . There are large numbers of liberal minds to which the new book will be a most welcome and helpful volume." — *Boston Transcript.*

"'Ecce Deus' leaves 'Ecce Homo' far behind, and casts a shade over it, as it rises to the higher and grander theme of the Incarnation. We are sorry we cannot enter into the merits of this work, but we advise our readers to peruse it along with 'Ecce Homo,' and they will be satisfied of the important part its author plays as a vindicator of 'the Truth as it is in Jesus.'" — *Scottish American Journal.*

THE SEER; or, Common Places Refreshed. By LEIGH HUNT. In two volumes, 16mo. Price, $3.00.

"A collection of delicious essays, thoroughly imbued with the characteristics of the writer's genius and manner, and on topics especially calculated to bring out all the charms of his genial spirit and develop all the niceties of his fluent diction, and worthy of being domesticated among those choice family books which while away leisure hours with agreeable thoughts and fancies." — *Boston Transcript.*

"The 'Seer' is one of the best specimens of the modern essayist's dealing with the minor pleasures and domestic philosophy of life, and is a capital antidote for the too exciting books of the hour; it lures us to musing, and what Hazlitt calls 'reposing on our sensations.'" — *H. T. Tuckerman.*

THE LIFE AND DEATH OF JASON. A Poem. By WILLIAM MORRIS. One volume, 16mo. Price, $1.50.

"In all the noble roll of our poets there has been since Chaucer no second teller of tales, no second rhapsode comparable to the first, till the advent of this one." — *A. C. Swinburne.*

"A poem remarkable for originality, freshness, and vividness of description, and beauty and force of narration." — *London Review.*

"In his style he exercises upon us the spells of the accomplished story-teller." — *Pall Mall Gazette.*

☞ *Mailed, post-paid, to any address, on receipt of the price, by the Publishers.*

www.ingramcontent.com/pod-product-compliance
Lightning Source LLC
Chambersburg PA
CBHW030304170426
43202CB00009B/867